bent street 3

Australian LGBTIQA+ arts, writing & ideas

Clouds of Magellan Press | Melbourne

Gay
Gay Aboriginal men are REAL Aboriginal men.
Aboriginal Australia was a queer history
REAL Aboriginal men.
Always was. Always will be. Aboriginal QUEER Mob!
QUEER is Beautiful
LGBTIQS + mob
Always was. Always will be.
QUEER his is beautiful
Ab Aboriginal Australia queer eer his
Always was. Always will be. Aboriginal QUEER Mob!
Gay Aboriginal men a
= LOVE

As well as the traditional owners of the land on which this exhibition is showing, I would also like to pay my respects to the gay, lesbian, transgender - brother boys and sister girls - intersex, queer and other rainbow Aboriginal and Torres Strait Islander people who have gone before me and made it possible for me to have this show. Thank you for your courage and for paving the way to this point. May our activism continue until we can all stand up with pride as Aboriginal queer mob, free from discrimination and hurt.

Peter Waples-Crowe
Acknowledgement
at InsideOUT, May 2019, Koorie Heritage Trust, Melbourne

Bent Street is published by Clouds of Magellan Press, Melbourne, www.cloudsofmagellanpress.net.

cloudsofmagellanpress@gmail.com

Bent Street welcomes contributions at any time. Visit bentstreet.net for submission details.

ISBN: (paperback) 978-0-6484604-8-0
ISBN: (ebook) 978-0-6484604-9-7

Editor: Tiffany Jones
Contributing editors: Ashley Sievwright, Gordon Thompson, Jodie Hare (UK)
Logo: Andrew Liu
Design: Gordon Thompson

Publication and distribution, Lightning Source, through eBook Alchemy—ebookalchemy.com

Cover: Jamie James | Nova Gina, Black Nulla, Koori Gras, Carriageworks 2019.

Back Cover: Jamie James | Workshop wall, development week, Koori Gras, Carriageworks 2019.

Section break images: Gordon Thompson | Colorado snow; Alcatraz kitchen—the knives are out; Bent St; Venice Beach carpark; Motel sign, Utah.

contents

2019: THE YEAR IN QUEER

POETRY

FICTION

Acknowledgments

Thankyou to: Alexis Desaulniers-Lea for the photo of Maude Davey and Mama Alto; Maude Davey supplied the image from the film *Elizabeth Taylor Sometimes* (prod. Liz Struth and Deb Baulch, Wild Iris Productions, 1996).

INTRODUCTION
TIFFANY JONES

Welcome back to *Bent Street*, a twisted tapestry of our time. In 2019 we have weavers well-known and new, spooling glittering gossamers into our web. We maintain a strong loom of redolent writers, poignant poets, enraged essayists and unflinching photographers. Nevertheless, for the first time we are now interlaced with gallant graphic novelists, defiant digital artists, and inspiring installation-artists. *Bent Street 3* stays focussed on its role as an 'annual' publication: featuring works from LGBTIQA+ and allied creators in 2019, themes arising from 2019, and the view backwards and forwards as at 2019.

Three thicker threads wend their way through the thinner filaments of this woven work. The first thread woven through our tapestry belongs to Australia's First Nations peoples: the strengthening of public displays of Aboriginal and Torres Strait Islander LGBTIQA+ pride and visibility was a major 2019 theme. From Koori Gras in February (see Jamie James' cover photo of Nova Gina, and Black Nulla Koori Gras Carriageworks photo essay); to Peter Waples-Crowe's Koorie Heritage Trust art exploring Ngarigo and queer identity showing in Melbourne in May. Indigenous Queer Studies academic, Andrew Farrell, a Wodi Wodi descendant from Jerrinja Aboriginal community on the South Coast of NSW, describes their development of world-first Aboriginal Queer University Units. Bee Cruse, born and bred on Cabrogal country (a clan within the Darug nation), whose family comes from the Gomeroi, Wiradjuri and Monaroo-Yuin peoples of NSW) describes a first experience of Koori Gras which brought deeper connections to family. Mandy Henningham discusses complications to Queer Indigenous research.

The second thread belongs to times of crisis: LGBTIQA+ people and our allies respond to ruination of our planet in the climate crisis and other types of crises. Michelle Bishop, a Gamilaroi woman from Western New South Wales (NSW) living on Dharawal Country south of Sydney, shares a poem about the devastatingly uncivilised impacts of so-called 'civilisation'. Xavier, a Black Australian university student not yet out to family and inspired by the Extinction Rebellion climate protection movement, shares a triptych of poems 'Colour's end' discussing the political and existential threats to the environment, queerness and people of colour. Jason Li writes of the crisis in Hong Kong, and how LGBTIQA+ people shape resistance cultures. Ayman Kaake's refugee-inspired photo-stories explore travelling by boat to Australia when one's own home is untenable. Lionel Wright watches his Mexican-American boyfriend's family crisis unfold under Trump Administration immigration clamp-downs. Stephanie Amir discusses feeling on the fringes whilst navigating the discovery of disabilities. The Year in Queer includes Randy Rainbow's cabaret covers and Toddrick Hall's power pop as hyper-queer snap-backs to various crises.

A third strand is the battle for religious accommodation of LGBTIQA+ people and women, as the line between freedom of religion and discrimination against LGBTIQA+ people was ferociously debated this year. Academics including Timothy Jones and Jennifer Power discuss the best pathways forward around Victorian and broader moves to ban LGBT conversion therapies. Clare Monagle offers a personal account of the fallout from the fall of Cardinal Pell in 'The Church Herself'. Geoff Allshorn discusses gay and atheist liberations. Jocelyn Deane's 'Trading Saints' triptych explores devotions, rituals and sacrifices. Young artist Hannah Buttsworth shares three artworks featured in the *Art Express* collection 'Renascence'; representing a growing awareness of identity while within a condemning religious environment and the catharsis of being oneself.

Bent Street 3 has many other cords curving through it from gender to romance. Wrap yourself in its fabric as a source of cover in battles, comfort in crisis, and the warmth of community …

Tiffany Jones—Editor
1 November 2019

FIRST PERSON

OUTSIDER. PETER WAPLES-CROWE

InsideOUT
PETER WAPLES-CROWE

Why am I constantly on the outside? I'm so familiar with that position that it's my go to, my stable, the way I see the world. I'm on the outside of the queer community because of my Ngarigo identity and I'm on the outside of the Aboriginal and Torres Strait Islander community because I'm queer. The Elders, from my experience, really hate the word Queer, because it has so many negative connotations for older people; but I'm really comfortable calling myself a queer Koori. I used to say gay but maybe gay is too soft or something. My thinking is queer and broader than just gay.

I'm also a Ngarigo person, not a Ngarigo *man*, that's all way too binary I feel now, and I need to be opening space up in the Community for trans- people and non-binary mob. We have a pretty rigid tradition of Men's Business and Women's Business and we need to make room. Cultures change and shift with time, they are not static things and maybe we need some new thinking around old modes of culture to create more space for the new.

InsideOUT is the name of a short documentary and the name of a solo art show that ran in May 2019 at the Koorie Heritage Trust in Melbourne, and some of my prints were displayed at the Original BOX show at Boomalli Art Gallery for the Mardi Gras in Sydney.

InsideOUT is the perfect title for me and really sums up my life in 2019. My art is from my inside, my livingness; but I'm very queer out and proud. I was adopted into a white family at birth and my journey back to my Ngarigo was from the outside to coming IN to the Community. That journey was made harder because I was queer, and it was already very tough and distressing at times. I thought it would be some linkup fantasy but no, it took me close to 25 years to find my connections in a real way and to settle my spirit. I was too busy being a queen really for the first part of my life in the AIDS era, which was enough for anyone to deal with. My Aboriginal journey came later and I'm so glad I survived both experiences and am strong and deadly today. I have my ancestors with me that's for sure. I'm so bloody lucky for that, but I do try to keep them close these days.

I'm known as Ngurran in my tribe which is the emu. And it a very apt animal for me because it bends the gender roles, with the male emu sitting on the eggs and raising the chicks. My Uncle gave me this name after he had a vision of an Emu sitting on a nest of eggs and carved on the eggs were pictures of Dingos. I think I really wanted the dingo as my name originally and was disappointed that I got the emu because I have painted *mirrigang* (wild dogs) all my life really and feel a close spiritual connection to all wild dogs. The dingo has come into focus in my art in recent years because I love using symbols, and to me the dingo is a marginalised native animal that in most parts of Australia is not protected, so it's become a queer person emblem. I'm a queer native and not afforded all the same rights as the rest of the natives. Like the dingo I am seen, by some, as a 'pest' and a 'nuisance' and I can be attacked or hunted, like the dingo is, by farmers who see it as a threat to their livelihood or their 'progress'.

Colonisation has not been kind to the dingo and it hasn't been kind to me and my people either.

I like that I am Ngurran and I love my Uncle's vision of me in the end. All I ever wanted was a place in the tribe. I love that I am a queer Ngarigo person and that our Country is the high snow Country and that we are the snow or ice people. I try to visit my Country when I can and this year I attended a small workshop about our language (Ngarigu), and who knows how it will influence my art and my life?

My journey back to country has been a long and often difficult one and home is not without its trauma; but I'm glad I am where I am and I look forward to learning more. I still feel my queerness puts me on the outside and I know other Aboriginal queer people who are not welcome in their tribes because of it. My partner has never come with me to meet my tribe so I guess that will be a test if it ever happens.

Alone I can dip in and out of Country but I still sometimes feel unsafe there. The last time I went back I heard lots of traumatic stories and it made me glad I don't live there all the time. I just don't need that, but I know my cousins are there on country representing me. I stay in touch over Facebook and keep track of people. I'm still like the Dingo, sometimes I want to be hanging with the Mob and other times I need my own space. I'm inside my tribe and I'm OUT, but it's still a balancing act.

CAMP OUT. PETER WAPLES-CROWE

Peter Waples-Crowe is an indigenous queer artist, involved in art production and health education. He lives in Melbourne. @pwcrowe insta @peterwaplescrowe

OUT ON THE FRINGES
STEPHANIE AMIR

My legs and hands become increasingly paralysed for three days and four nights before I decide to go to a doctor. By then my feet are cold, lifeless lumps. Bending my knees even slightly causes my legs to sear with pain and collapse, but somehow it is not until my hands are too weak to pick up my morning cup of coffee that I admit to myself that something is very wrong.

In the emergency ward, I have blood tests and muscle tests and a test for the flu. Later the doctor orders a lumbar puncture, which involves sticking a giant needle between my vertebrae to extract spinal fluid. He asks me to curl into a ball and hold still.

To keep my mind off the pain I focus on memories of doubles-trapeze training, imagining myself bracing my abdominal muscles and holding tight to the forearms of my flyer so she won't fall. Surely if I can flip a woman through the air, I can hold tight in a ball.

Twenty minutes later, the neurologist comes in with my diagnosis. 'You have Guillain-Barré Syndrome.'

'Nah,' I say, trying to be funny. 'I ordered an acute potassium deficiency, so that you could give me one injection and my legs would work again.'

'Well,' he responds with a raised eyebrow. 'We'd narrowed it down to Guillain-Barré, Multiple Sclerosis or spinal tumours, so from that list you got the pick of the bunch—at least you'll recover.'

Not everyone does recover from Guillain-Barré. It's an autoimmune illness that attacks the nerves and the myelin sheaths that protect them, causing 'ascending paralysis' that starts in the hands and feet then gradually ascends up the body over hours, days or weeks. For some people, their whole body, including their lungs, become completely paralysed. There's no reliable cure, so it's mostly just a matter of keeping the patient alive until the acute phase is over, then months of rehab while the myelin sheaths grow back. Most people survive, but usually their bodies don't go back to how they were before.

I went to sleep in the Intensive Care Unit as the paralysis crept through my thighs and across my hips, through my fingers and towards my wrists. I could still move my arms and torso, but knew that by morning they might be cut off from my brain too.

An hour later, I woke up freezing cold and shaking violently, my blood pressure plummeting. Terrified, I cried out and begged the nurse for more blankets. She turned off the drip (intravenous immunoglobulins, an immune-system transplant) and gave me some kind of opioid.

Eventually the shaking stopped. As my body temperature returned to normal I felt hot under the mountain of blankets and absent-mindedly kicked them off. The nurse and I both looked at the blankets, then my legs, then each other. Then I was crying again, but this time with relief. The nurse said in twenty years working in ICU, she'd never seen such a quick turnaround of a Guillain-Barré patient.

I thought the worst was over, and the most dangerous part was, but I'd entered a messier, more enduring stage. My friend Ben came to visit me and quipped: 'You're already a young queer woman with a baby and a Middle Eastern name. You didn't need to add 'disability' to your list of minority groups.'

When I got home from hospital, dinners arrived on our doorstep each evening. At first, showering and dressing used up almost my entire day's energy so I spent the rest of it lying down and reading on the bed, couch or banana-lounge. I couldn't parent beyond letting my eight-month-old crawl on or around me, so was totally reliant on my partner. A month later I was tanned from the banana-lounging and able to hobble around the house. 'You don't look sick,' some friends said, meaning it as a compliment. But I was. I couldn't even stand up to wash the dishes without collapsing in a feverish heap.

Two months after leaving hospital my in-laws visited from Canberra and we went on a daytrip to Healesville Sanctuary, because we knew my daughter would love the bird show. I still couldn't stand for more than a few minutes at a time so we borrowed a wheelchair. People smiled appreciatively at my father-in-law as he pushed me around, but either ignored me or gave a well-intended but infantilising smile, like someone might give a small child sitting obediently in her pram.

Those patronising smiles jarred with my sense of self, and I wondered how long other wheelchair-users lasted before yelling at people. 'This isn't all that I am!' I was tempted to shout, 'I'm a politician and community leader! I was elected with the highest primary vote in my ward! I am responsible for millions of dollars of public infrastructure! I've already fulfilled five of my six election commitments in my first year! LOOK, I CAN SHOW YOU OUR STRATEGIC PLAN ON MY PHONE RIGHT NOW!!'

Instead I stayed quiet. Rationally I knew that a person's worth wasn't related to their career achievements. Yet despite my frustration at the stereotyped expectations of what a person with a disability should look like or how they should act, I felt bound to fulfil them. On the days I was out in a wheelchair, I felt like I shouldn't stand up in case someone thought I was 'faking it'. When I returned to work I used a walking-stick, not because it made walking easier but because I was convinced that otherwise no one would believe I really *did* need the tram seat, or to sit down for the duration of any networking function.

I felt disabled in the sense that I was not physically able to live as I did before, but also didn't feel disabled 'enough' to consider myself a 'real' person with a disability. It started to mess with my head. Seeking clarity I messaged my friend Brigid, who has albinism and also understands people and humanity in a deep way that I, as a science-minded feelings-phobe, do not.

'Oh, everyone feels like that,' she said. 'I feel like that. I have a mate who has cerebral palsy and most other people would consider her to have really significant disabilities but she still feels on the fringes of the disability community.' I didn't know how to respond. The idealistic part of my brain couldn't get past the principle of equity of access for everyone including access to community and collective identity, but the logical part wondered whether inclusion in a community required active participation and contribution. Meanwhile the frightened part of my brain resisted any challenge to my former identity.

Brigid—astute as always—shifted to a frame I'd understand better.

'Imagine if a young bisexual woman came to you, as someone active in the LGBTIQ community, and said 'I don't deserve to be here because I only came out a few months ago, and I don't feel like I'm gay enough'. What would you say to her?'

'I'd say that that LGBTIQ community is for all LGBTIQ people, regardless of how long they've been out or who they've been with or how they identify,' I responded.

It seemed too obvious to even bother articulating.
I mused over this in the months that followed. I'd held leadership roles in the LGBTIQ community for more than a decade and had

been proud of promoting inclusion across the spectrums, but the more I thought about it, looked around me and spoke to friends and colleagues, the more I realised how—unlike me—many people in Melbourne's LGBTIQ community felt on the fringes. I started listing the people I knew who have said they didn't feel like they belonged: there were people who identified more strongly with other parts of themselves, people who felt like they were 'too young' or 'too old' to fit in, people with a culture or religion other than Anglo-atheism, people who couldn't afford to go out to queer events, people for whom it's not safe to come out, neurodiverse people, pretty much anyone identifying with the letters beyond the 'LG' part of the alphabet-list, and many more.

That didn't leave many people in the middle, who felt that they belonged within the LGBTIQ community. Perhaps this meant there were even more LGBTIQ people at the fringes than in the centre. What did that mean for our community? What did it mean for any community?

I am still contemplating those questions, but I guess it just means that we all continue to live loudly and proudly—or equally valid: quietly and contentedly—from the centre of some circles and the edges of others. Inclusion is a collective responsibility, while identity is an individual decision; both contribute to the creation of culture within communities.

According to the neurologist's definition, I have 'recovered' from Guillain-Barré. I can now walk, run and work fulltime, but my legs start shaking and my brain stops working properly if I sit or stand for too long, and there's no way my hands or abdominal muscles are strong enough to return to doubles-trapeze.

I now directly tell people that I have a disability, and the reaction is almost identical to when I tell people that I'm gay. Often they flinch or raise their eyebrows in surprise, so slightly that it's almost hidden, but not quite. Then they try to say something supportive while rapidly scanning their memories for anything accidentally-offensive or exclusionary that they might have ever said to me. Usually it's ok. The awkwardness is the price I pay to be myself, and to improve visibility for the sake of others living at the fringes.

Being confronted with the decision of whether to embrace or reject my new identity as a person with a disability has reminded me that it's not a binary decision: the strength with which we hold each of our identities is different for each person, and maybe even each day. Currently I am very queer, slightly disabled, a proud mum, a somewhat successful local politician, and a totally useless trapeze artist.

I bet one of those labels made you flinch, just slightly.

Stephanie Amir is a public health researcher and elected local councillor. She has been actively involved in the LGBTIQ community for many years including as a radio presenter and on the Board of Directors at LGBTIQ radio station JOY 94.9, Program Manager for Safe Schools Coalition Australia, inaugural Co-Convenor of Queer Greens Victoria, and Chair of the Sex, Sexuality and Gender Diversity community advisory committee at the City of Darebin. She lives in Melbourne with her partner and daughter.

BROOKE LYNN HYTES. MEL SIMPSON

MEL SIMPSON

Mel Simpson works on both commercial and fine art projects. Her commercial work is predominantly focused on queer popular culture from Australia and abroad, with a particular drag queen and camp tv slant, while her fine art content is influenced by sexuality, gender identity and nature.

PREVIOUS PAGE: BROOKE LYNN HYTES. MEL SIMPSON

FOLLOWING PAGES: GENTLEMAN JACK, SAD DRUMMERS CLUB, ALYSSA EDWARDS, KATE MCKINNON

Born and raised in Queensland, Mel Simpson received a Bachelor of Fine Art from Griffith University in 2006, majoring in painting. She moved to Melbourne the following year and has been a Melbourne dweller ever since, with the exception of a year living in Vancouver, Canada. Mel has exhibited in solo and group shows in Queensland, New South Wales and Victoria, including shows for Midsumma at galleries such as Gasworks, 69 Smith Street and Red Gallery. More recently she has started her own independent illustration business, Kittenpants Studios.

GENTLEMAN JACK. MEL SIMPSON

SAD DRUMMERS CLUB. MEL SIMPSON

ALYSSA EDWARDS. MEL SIMPSON

KATE MCKINNON. MEL SIMPSON

INTERVIEW
ANDREW FARRELL

Indigenous Queer Studies academic, Andrew Farrell, talks with *Bent Street* editor Tiffany Jones about their development of world-first Aboriginal Queer University Units. Andrew Farrell is a Wodi Wodi person and Queer identified academic whose research is focused on LGBTIQA+ Aboriginal peoples and social media. Andrew has also developed projects such as the *Archiving the Aboriginal Rainbow* blog, an online portal that addresses the absence of a digital space that catalogues Aboriginal and Torres Strait Islander sexual and gender diversity by sharing links to contemporary and historical audio, images, articles, art, and various other items found across the web (Farrell, 2014). The blog prioritises the perspectives of Indigenous LGBTIQ+ peoples as decolonising agents within Nakata's (2007, in Farrell, 2015) 'Cultural Interface'—in which Indigenous LGBTIQ knowledge, experiences and challenges filter through complex terrains of knowing and unknowing—transforming how we may see and know this unique and diverse community. *Bent Street* caught up with Andrew Farrell to discuss their latest contribution in developing and co-ordinating world-first units in Aboriginal Queer Studies commencing in 2020 at Macquarie University.

Tiffany Jones: Tell us about your role at Macquarie?

Andrew Farrell: I am both a PhD student here at Macquarie as well as a lecturer/tutor. I am in a fellowship position which is made up of largely tutoring, lecturing, and research projects within my department. It has given me the opportunity to advance my academic qualifications and undertake new and exciting roles, such as designing courses, lectures, and conference speaking while at the same time building my own specialised area of research. It's a fabulous fluid space!

As an undergraduate student, I had a lot of growing pains to work through in finding my academic career path. Moving into an honours and deciding to undertake a PhD housed within Indigenous Studies I have found a place to thrive, create, and find my place in academia. It works alongside my family obligations. I wear many hats! The

Macquarie fellowship role fits into that lifestyle as its flexibility facilitates the shifting demands of learning, teaching, and cultural life.

Tiffany Jones: What new ground are you adding to Indigenous LGBTIQ+ academia in this role? Or, do you find, your work is in adding to the ground itself?

Andrew Farrell: I am adding to the developing stages of this field of inquiry. There is some academic work in the field but it is sparse. I see it as a space full of opportunity… the word 'potential' comes to mind! Between and across the humanities are these 'potentially' overlapping fields of knowledge to explore: LGBTIQ+ Studies, Indigenous Studies, Gender Studies and so on. These overlapping spaces are a reflection of the realities of being Indigenous and Queer and relating to multiple communities—Indigenous communities, LGBTIQ+ communities, and Indigenous LGBTIQ+ communities. My work is about acknowledging these dynamics and undertaking projects that flow between fields and bringing new challenges to established fields of inquiry—Indigenising Queer Studies and Queering Indigenous Studies.

Tiffany Jones: Speaking of doing Queer differently, your article 'Lipstick Clapsticks: A yarn and a Kiki with an Aboriginal drag queen' (Farrell, 2016) provides a very personalised introduction of Indigenous themes in Queer writing. Tell us about the importance of yarns and kikis?

Andrew Farrell: These are both cultural and colloquial terms used across Indigenous and LGBTIQ+ communities. We, Aboriginal peoples, use the word 'yarn' to describe how we relate to each-other on an interpersonal level within Aboriginal communities. Coming from the Queer community—particularly the Black and Latin Queer communities in the US—the term 'kiki' refers to interpersonal queer relationships. I use those terms to basically say 'I trust and acknowledge you as my kin: you are my friend, sister or brother'.

Interestingly, these terms are not necessarily gendered. Yarning does not imply or describe particular gendered interaction. Having a kiki also brings additional meaning to the already de-gendered interpersonal connection. I wanted to bring these ideas together to reflect my involvement in multiple cultural, social, and political arenas to signal my identity across both. I also used both terms to invite people from Queer and Indigenous communities to feel they could lean in and observe a snapshot of my life as both Queer and Indigenous.

My PhD thesis is looking at LGBTIQ Indigenous people on social media. As an Indigenous researcher, I have a responsibility to identify my position within these communities first in order to then undertake further research. As an Aboriginal person it is always necessary to start with identifying who you are, what community and culture you belong to. As I contribute to the LGBTIQ Indigenous space I want to reassure mob that it is a Queer identified Aboriginal person doing the research rather than an outsider looking in.

Tiffany Jones: Would you like to tell our readers a little bit more about how you identify?

Andrew Farrell: Sure. I come from the Jerrinja Aboriginal community on the South Coast of NSW. I identify as Queer as I like the potential and ambiguity in that word. Growing up I have identified as gay, gender-fluid, non-binary … and just kind of ended up at the term Queer. Where I am from I didn't always have the language to articulate that, so it has taken me some time to finally say that I am Queer.

I knew that I was different as a child but it wasn't until my university years that I began to seek out and identify as gender and sexually diverse. To give some context, this happened through undergraduate years in visual arts doing sculpture, drawing, a tiny bit of painting. My artistic practices moved with me into drag, in which I became involved with my local LGBTIQ+ scene. Being involved with the Queer student community, I was able to finally discuss what being 'gay' meant and what further possibilities I could explore in terms of gender. I think all of that has been important in determining my path, both positive and negative. As I came to terms with my gender and sexuality I also felt further isolation from my Aboriginal community because these ideas, these ways of identifying, are not understood and thereby not fully accepted.

I still have a lot of wonderful relationships with my community. They have not let go of me, and I have not let go of them. Our cultural ties are strong enough to withstand these kinds of differences for the most part. I am not discouraged by these challenges but I want to navigate them as safely as possible. It is hard work and it has taken a lot out of me. I have only reached my 30s but I am the first born in my mother's side of my family, so I have never known a time where I did not have many responsibilities to my family.

These challenges have informed my priorities for where I want to go in my career, starting with my family. For Aboriginal academics, our priorities often start with maintaining our families and communities. As a Queer person that must also account for the specific challenges and experiences of this intersecting and complex social and cultural space.

Tiffany Jones: Yes, for queer academics our work can be very emotionally entwined with our experiences and our drive to reflect or impact them. Is there some area where you especially feel a drive to make an impact in particular?

Andrew Farrell: I personally would like to see improvements in the self-worth and value of Queer Indigenous people. I want them to be valued, loved, supported, and given opportunities to participate and have their say. I definitely have issues with my self-worth and value based on the trauma that I have experienced in relation to my identity. I want people to be able to feel it is okay to be both Indigenous and Queer. I don't aim to be a role model and am not confident enough to say 'I stand for particular values' or to have people comparing themselves to me, but to know there are many parts of myself that may have relevance and value to others identifying in a similar way or ways. I don't like to set limits on myself; I think that is the main thing. If I stand to represent anything I want it to reflect that diversity is possible.

Tiffany Jones: This position of a non-position or anti-answer, where it is not so much about presenting a specific example but not putting limits on identities that are possible, is in some ways the very best of Queer's offerings! A frustrating thing is when Queer is accidentally authoritarian.

Andrew Farrell: Yes! It is my responsibility as an Aboriginal Queer person in academia to be cautious and promote diversity for all of its offerings and understand its pitfalls. One of my biggest worries is the issue of gatekeeping around identity as it exists across and between multiple communities. Drawing from Indigenous LGBTIQ+ standpoints we can begin to discuss these issues. What it means to be Queer and Aboriginal in a settler-colonial state is deeply political and pushes multiple boundaries, norms, and so on. We need to challenge and unpack these topics and reassert existing ways of thinking to push the boundaries on issues such as racism, queerphobia, heteronormativity, and various prevalent social issues. Queer Indigenous perspectives may seem new to a lot of people but our existence is entrenched in ancient and living cultures. In our classes we will discuss the rise of marginalised peoples, face issues such as acceptance, and examine how both the Indigenous and LGBTIQ community is implicated.

Tiffany Jones: Are there other cultural terms or ideas you draw on?

Andrew Farrell: As far as incorporating cultural ideas, we will do that throughout our course content. We are currently building the thematic flow for our units. All of them rest in similar politics of wanting to revive Indigenous ways of knowing, not to say these are dead or dormant, but to demonstrate that they are valued, viable, and critical contributions to knowledge about gender and sexual diversity.

In the Australian context, it is important to include, for example, Aboriginal and Torres Strait Islander transgender communities' use of terms like 'Sistergirl' and 'Brotherboy' which uniquely identifies being both transgender and Indigenous. These terms have utility across this vastly diverse continent which is home to over 250 distinct Indigenous language (and cultural) groups in Australia. In that regard I aim to respect the unique, distinct, and varied genders and sexualities of Aboriginal and Torres Strait cultures in the exact same way I would aim to value and respect the diversity of international Indigenous cultures, and bring to light conversations that tie these margins together.

Many Indigenous cultures around the globe are reasserting the importance of culturally informed and self-determined gender and sexual diversities. Whether these voices are from here in Australia, Two-Spirit peoples in Turtle Island (US & Canada), and Takatāpui in Aotearoa (New Zealand), LGBTIQ+ Indigenous cultural resurgence is gaining visibility and traction across the globe. My role, and the work of Queer Indigenous Studies, is to recognise this heterogeneity and mobilise it against oppressive forces, beginning in the classroom.

Tiffany Jones: Is there an aspect of decolonising work in Australian Queer context that engages with Aboriginal and Torres Strait Islander diversity, in breaking away from British punitive approaches to homosexuality for example, in the way that this frame seems to be called upon in South African or other colonised nations?

Andrew Farrell: From the outset, Aboriginal and Torres Strait Islander peoples challenge to settler colonialism is, in part, about maintaining our cultural autonomy and rights. Gender and sexuality have always been components of that struggle.

We have been significantly impacted by dominant representations of our peoples. We have been forced into the gender binary. Through my personal experience categories interpreted as 'men and women's business' do not reflect the lived realities and complexities in my culture. I view them as rigid and imposed assumptions about our societies which have had a significant impact on us. It has reimagined us for the sole purpose of control … the coloniser told us that 'this is who we were, and this is who we should be'.

Against that, it has been important for me to resist by, for example, acknowledging that my grandmother was the head of our household! That we continue to function upon what I can only articulate as a *matriarchal* system! Even where power balances and imbalances are present they do not sit within a Western gender binary paradigm. Aboriginal women are and will always be powerful! Much of that power rests in the relationality of Indigenous society. It is impressive, but not surprising, Aboriginal women continue to navigate the challenges of settler-colonial patriarchy while maintaining culturally distinct forms of leadership.

While we continue to assert our strength, the Queer community in Australia must recognise historical injustices and work against the ways that they may perpetuate ideas about Indigenous peoples as guests and benefactors of settler colonialism. There are a range of issues to discuss within the context of Queer movements and I think a good starting place is building a literacy and awareness of the issues that play out and challenging them.

Tiffany Jones: Yes! There can be comparatively less power for women within the Colonising Discourse and systems of rule in Australia. If you think of how much women in top roles such as Julie Bishop for example— as recently one of the most powerful women within its systems—said she struggled to be accepted in a role of power, it is quite striking. She couldn't stay in that role in power, and talked in interviews about how she struggled at first with expressing her femininity, hid herself in a kind of masculine coding just to be there, and had to at all times hide any feeling

of ambition … It's interesting how Indigenous societies, that have been
here for so much longer, empower Indigenous womens' leadership.

Andrew Farrell: Bishop's example is a reminder that patriarchy and
settler colonialism is in full force. This system needs to be challenged.
There is a lot to learn from Aboriginal cultures through the one
example of women. Pushing that further there is also a lot to learn
from Aboriginal transgender women; women who explicitly resist
essentialist and colonial ideas about womanhood while also
performing cultural obligations as Aboriginal women. Aboriginal
women face the colonial regime and subvert it in ways that empower
the community as a whole. It is beyond the scope of what has been
identified as a weakness in feminism identified as 'white feminism.'
Aboriginal scholars such as Aileen Moreton-Robinson have been
critical in the identification and criticism of patriarchy in tandem with
colonialism in Australia, which now must account for positions
beyond the gender binary. These are the kinds of critical inquiry we
will undertake in our courses.

Tiffany Jones: Are these courses that anyone can take? Do you need to
mediate what you put into the course to protect certain groups or
knowledges?

Andrew Farrell: In designing these courses we're constantly
navigating ethical issues such as accessibility, accountability, care and
responsibility. We're very much mindful of the limitations of work we
can and should include across LGBTIQ+ Indigenous topics. One of
the features of our courses will be having guest lecturers who consent
to sharing their expertise and experience through lectures and
resources. There is a dearth of historical resources on the topic more
broadly, however in recent years there has been a resurgence of
articles, books, and all manner of text which represent the experiences
of Indigenous LGBTIQ + people in this country. I aim to hand the
platform to as many people across our communities with the
resources I have available to me.

Tiffany Jones: Yes, there is an element of care-taking in how we present
our communities. Also for example we can have young queer people be
just so overly generous with their information in ways that do not look
after themselves in times where their identities are politicised, so we may
hold back some of their information that they may just hand out freely in

a publication without understanding the impact (things like phone numbers or personal details they don't need 'out there')!

Andrew Farrell: Yes. Indigenous Queer Studies in Australia is new ethical ground. In my own experience of putting together human ethics applications for my work I have faced issues such as ethics boards not having experience in the ethical terrains of multiple minority groups. There are not necessarily people within the system who know exactly what constitutes best ethical practice for LGBTIQ+ Indigenous peoples. I have to magnify and intensify being self-critical, for example, in how I go about seeking data from the community. This increased pressure is also a reflection of my personal integrity to the ethics process and responsibility to community. As this field grows, we will need to have people in the system who are capable and qualified.

Tiffany Jones: The inclusion of these communities in research is highly sensitive. For outsiders, there is a feeling of not wanting to do the wrong thing. Do you think the work should be led by Aboriginal Queer people?

Andrew Farrell: I think that Indigenous LGBTIQ+ peoples should be at the helm of all research relating to them. I also think that non-Indigenous and/or non-queer researchers have a responsibility to engage with the research and use their privileges to join us in the expanding of research into this field. I am already in contact with undergraduate students, both Indigenous and non-Indigenous, queer and non-queer, who are interested in this field of research, some of whom may go into the future as researchers who may contribute to the field.

Across Australian universities I have noticed little representation of LGBTIQ+ Aboriginal gender and sexuality topics in curriculum, for example, in womens studies, Indigenous studies, and across the broader Arts and Humanities. Often times Indigenous gender and sexuality topics are situated within the 'narratives of the nation' or 'the making of Australia' … and Aboriginal LGBTIQ voices are seldom included. We are making space to address those absences within the institution. The onus to get this field of study up and running will, as most areas of study based on marginalised peoples, be through the labour of that marginalised group.

Tiffany Jones: Exactly! And it is so exciting that you are bringing such units into being, can you tell our readers about them?

Andrew Farrell: As it currently stands, we are moving forward with three Indigenous Queer units of study which will be available on campus and through Open Access Universities.

Next year, in 2020, we are starting ABST1030 (Introduction to Indigenous Queer Studies). It is an introductory course that focuses in on Aboriginal and Torres Strait Islander gender and sexual diversities, perspectives, and issues in Australia.

Then we will have ABST2035 (Global Indigenous Queer Identities). It is a course that is made up of international case studies. We will explore LGBTIQ+ Indigenous case studies in Australia, Aotearoa (New Zealand) and the Pacific region, and Turtle Island (US and Canada). This course is about important global conversations and connections.

The third is ABST3035 (Indigenous Queer Theory and Practice). It operates on a much more theoretical level. It will be a dense, in-depth course for students to explore ideas such as intersectionality, violence, decolonisation, and so on.

Tiffany Jones: I love that! It's a fantastic progression. So then studying these courses, what do people need to be enrolled in?

Andrew Farrell: At this point the first unit is accessible to students wanting to take it as an elective across Australia. We will deliver it both on campus and to students nationwide through Open Universities. I think it would be good to be able to tailor the course to flexible learning rather than limiting it to only those privileged to be able to study on campus.

Having the course online is a response to modern living. We are all online! I place a lot of value in online learning as I have found, through the internet, the ability to network with my community and have found resources online which have significantly shaped my research. I have learned the value of text outside of the ivory tower of paywalled journal articles and expensive textbooks.

Tiffany Jones: It's an activist act to use those texts as well … it's where that knowledge is and where knowledge is heading, it makes ideas accessible to more people and changes the valuing process in academia.

Andrew Farrell: As a student and academic fellow I am doing my thesis by publication. While an odd path, it has given me a lot of insight into academic research. I am also doing a thesis by publication to test how I can potentially make my work more accessible as the community is largely outside of the academy. I wish to find some way to produce my work where the community is. It is not uncommon to see Indigenous LGBTIQ+ content produced online in Queer news sites, social media, and Indigenous media such as *Koorimail* and *IndigenousX*, so we need to follow the community and see what the community uses to depict themselves.

Tiffany Jones: We've taken so much of your time but is there anything else you wanted to say?

Andrew Farrell: I think what I wanted to emphasise is the support underpinning what I do. I think that it is important to have allies who function as 'accomplices'; people who take risks, who use whatever is afforded them to lend a hand to others.

At Macquarie I have been given a space to expand Indigenous Queer Studies through the Indigenous Studies Department which is led by Professor Bronwyn Carlson. She has been a mentor to me for many years now. Her vision for Indigenous Studies and research is to open it up to diverse Indigenous perspectives. She wants to see Indigenous Studies expand into new and exciting territories. We have this in common.

I am ready to explore all that this future has in store. I know there will be backlash and future challenges but I also know that I have the support to be unapologetically Queer and Aboriginal.

References

Farrell, A. (2014). Archiving the Aboriginal Rainbow. Accessed on 4.1.17.
Retrieved from: https://indigblackgold.wordpress.com/

Farrell, A. (2015). 'Can You See Me? Queer Margins in Aboriginal
Communities', *Journal of Global Indigeneity*, 1(1). Accessed on 15.1.16.
Retrieved from:
http://ro.uow.edu.au/cgi/viewcontent.cgi?article=1010&context=jgi

Farrell, A. (2016). Lipstick Clapsticks: A yarn and a Kiki with an Aboriginal
drag queen. *AlterNative*, 12(5). pp.574-585.

Farrell, A. (2017). Archiving the Aboriginal Rainbow: Building an Aboriginal
LGBTIQ Portal. *Australasian Journal of Information Systems*, 21(1). pp.2-
14.

Andrew Farrell is an Indigenous Early Career Academic Fellow in the
Department for Indigenous Studies, Macquarie University. Andrew is a
Wodi Wodi descendant from Jerrinja Aboriginal community on the South
Coast of NSW. Their research is multidisciplinary with a focus on
Aboriginal LGBTIQ gender and sexualities, media and online studies, and
drag performance. Andrew is also undertaking a PhD project titled
Aboriginal LGBTIQ peoples online. You can find their online blog at
https://indigblackgold.wordpress.com/

GREETING CARD 1. ASHLEY SIEVWRIGHT

THE PRINCE OF REDFERN
BEE CRUSE

An idea sparks, awakening a slow burning flame …

Late in the warm month of February 2017 was the week-long Mardi Gras of the black fella persuasion; a safe space for us mob to come and socialise, party and be recognised in the queer scene of Sydney in the week leading up to Mardi Gras itself. All the black queers with their glitter beards and sequin dresses with fabulous wigs took over Redfern in style!

My first experience of Koori Gras was celebrated with my family; Aunty Kim, Aunty Lizzy and cousin Meriki. My fabulous cousin was fresh off the plane back from London (I was cheering because it meant not being 'the only queer in the village' at family bbqs!), and her mum had invited me out to party with them. 'For this new black, queer week', she described it.

It was Opening Night at 107 for Koori Gras; Exhibition and Performance. A whole week of black, LGBTQI, rainbow, beautiful peoples! As an up and coming baby dyke from the Western Suburbs trying to make a name in Redfern—*mmhmm, yes please*—I was *so* there!

I remember Aunty Kim in her bob-cut, pink wig, stylin' up with Aunty Lizzy. I was in my all black, lesbian uniform look (as usual) and the night was ours! I hadn't seen Aunty Kim dance like that in ages.

Over the week we saw black, queer history in the exhibition space at 107, conversed about several issues facing our communities over a shared a meal at Black Point, partied hard all week (I remember Meriki peeling me off her couch after Opening Night). We made some lifelong friends amongst all the razzle dazzle. Being with my beautiful family gave me the strength to get out there and meet new people, I had the confidence to be 100% myself in a public space … that's a rare feeling!

In a time of 'diversity' and people being 'politically correct' there still are groups in society that face immense discrimination and prejudice because of who they are, especially the Indigenous and LGBTQI communities. But I tell you what … I was in amongst our black, queer peoples that week, and I'd never felt so connected and free in my life!

I digress. The real highlight of Koori Gras was Friday night's 'Black Nulla', a fabulous spectacle for all black rainbow children everywhere! In the spirit of the night, I felt so connected to all my brothers and sisters.

Then, for the first time in my life, my eyes witnessed a whole line up of black Drag Queenz. A marvellous array of Black Royalty taking over the joint:

> Nova Gina
> Destiny Haz Arrived
> Miss Ellaneous
> Nanna Miss Koori, and
> Lacey Donovan.

It was enthralling. From the wigs, makeup and costumes, to the attitude, glamour and pizzazz. The way those Queens strut around that stage and made it their own, just *wow*. I even had my first lap dance—by none other than Nanna Miss Koori!

All with my family right beside me.

It's an overused phrase, but I felt like a kid in a candy store. My eyes couldn't get enough of everything I was taking in. And that's what Koori Gras is. It is more than a week-long event, or a time or place; it's a feeling of family, of connection and understanding. To come as you are, in all its glory; bold, blackness and Fabulous-ness! I think something was planted in me that night, a stirring. An idea.

A King is Born

The second year of Koori Gras (2018) I was invited by the Producer, Liza-Mare Syron, to attend the performance workshops run by Cherish Violet Blood. I know that I read the poster as 'performance workshop' but my heart took it as 'drag workshop'. The workshops were held during the week of Koori Gras, Cherish was teaching us about the craft of stage performance and how to 'find your stage character'—or as I took it, how to find my Drag persona!

When day 1 of the workshops came, I came to slay. I had a whole year to think about this moment. With inspirations and ideas flooding my brain, I knew I had something strong to go off! I was close to my grandfather, Pop Chop, when he was alive and he loved Prince. Pop's favourite song was 'Cream' (believe it or not). An ode to Pop Chop, Prince was my inspiration for my first show. I had to calm down a bit in order to be able to meet the 3 other participants, Buna, Katie and Simone. Then I met Cherish and her partner Lacey, who both whipped us into shape with vocal training, acting skills, amusing acting games that get you thinking on your feet and several other mind f*cking activities that get you out of your comfort zone and into the world of exploration! A magical, wonderful place for the artist to discover, play and find new ideas. And with that, we were off.

Amongst all the fun and games, we had the opportunity to develop a performance for the Black Nulla Cabaret to be held later that week. I think we all knew where I was going with my performance piece *cue the confetti guns … *DRAG KING*! Buna already had his amazing gothic, magician/siren character and Simone is a killer comedian with a great life story to back it up, she tells the best yarns! Katie told her story of being a black, queer, Catholic through the character of a painted up [in ochre], queer nun, habit and all.

These three participants are performers, they are used to being on stage. I was nervous because I was not a performer (I still don't regard myself as one), I'm not used to being in the spotlight. I must admit, I do face a bit of anxiety so I had all kinds of fears pulsing through my brain that week. Especially because I was exploring the drag persona of a very outgoing, sleazy, overzealous, but sexy and Fabulous man! Someone completely different to who I am in my daily life.

Those artists in that space gave me so much love and support that it gave me the confidence to find my Drag King persona … and along with it, my Drag Name: *Bee Dazzled Shanks—The Prince of Redfern. A bold and beautiful man, over confident and sleazily charming.*

I had a lot of homework. I was practicing pick-up lines, strutting like I've never strutted before through the halls of our rehearsal space. I was loud and took up space. All good traits of an overzealous male Drag persona.

The night before Black Nulla, I remember my little sister watching me trying out different styled glitter beards, she was six then and let's just say, there was glitter everywhere. We both successfully found our glitter beard styles.

Held at Carriageworks that year, Black Nulla Cabaret was bigger and better than ever! A spectacular night! All the black Drag Queens from the previous year came back to light up the stage and wow us all again. I remember all of us getting ready back stage, so many suit cases with all the necessities of fashionista Drag Queens. Glitter everywhere (mainly on my part) and just big hugs and support all round. All the beautiful queer, black family from the year before came back to party too, in numbers. It was so good catching up with friends and queer family I haven't seen in a while. And whilst I threw cream all over myself (to the fabulous musical workings of Prince— Cream) with a bit of a bump and grind along the stage, in a black latex diamante-fied G-string … *full disclosure:* I wore long black pants underneath the G-string.

I heard my family laughing and having a ball. My mum actually made me nervous cause I heard her laughing from backstage for the act before mine. I strut onto that stage with my family backing me, I had the love and support of our mob to give me the strength. Unfortunately, my Aunty Kim couldn't be there that night in the flesh, but when Aunty Lizzy hugged me at the end of my performance and said, 'Aunty Kim would be proud of you, she was here with us watching in pride', I cried.

Back with Black up

When Liza-Mare, asked me to come and perform for a second year … I was cheering! A comeback for Bee Dazzled Shanks—The Prince of Redfern at Koori Gras Black Nulla Cabaret! *Where do I sign?*

Unfortunately, I was flat out with my work and I found it hard to commit to the workshops but I heard (through the grapevine) that they were amazing! From costume design and making, to makeup and Drag workshops. I was jealous of the pics on the socials from the week. But when we were finally able to come into the rehearsal space and meet the other participants it was unbelievably fabulous! There were feathers and hats, feathers in hats, and prop guns, and an oversize teddy bear in the corner. Plus make-up, wigs, duct tape and a pink shirt with Yumi Stynes on it. This year's participants were on another level! This was going to be fun!

Armed with a weapon I did not have the previous year, I had my amazing partner Lou standing right beside me. True God, she's a gun. Lou and I share a love for a lot of the same music, and whilst chatting over some mad tunes we joked about her making a little cameo for my next show. Lou was reluctant, until later when we were short a drag queen. I was playing around with an idea of doing something to

'Pony' by Ginuwine, known as the Magic Mike song, with its seductive rhythms and addictive beats, but it was only an idea. I had nothing solid in it. Lou, a former Mardi Gras Party Director, pitched to me:

> *Imagine this. You are the cowboy and you work the stage with two drag queen horses; a black one and a white one. We mix the music from 'White Horse' (Wonderland Avenue) to 'Pony', the black horse can kick the white horse off the stage and you can get down to Pony with the black horse.*

Lou was in full production wife mode, I LOVED IT!

I knew I wanted to work with Felicia Foxx, and we were also looking for a big build drag queen I could potentially ride in on. But as time got away from us, and we didn't find our other butch queen (I even asked my tank Tongan brother-in-law if he'd give it a go … a solid 'no' from him). But the show must go on! Felicia and I started rehearsing. When Felicia heard the thumping, very 80s, high-tech disco machine track that is 'White Horse', well, she was the white horse. Lou, now crowned 'Daddy Cool' by 'Bee Dazzled Shanks', played the black horse, instead of being ridden in, he was led in. YAY! So, the story of the number changed a bit, the white horse got to stay.

Now, #realtalk. People concerned about that metaphor change of the white horse *seemingly* winning, don't worry. The black horse removed itself with utmost dignity and integrity whilst the white horse frantically threw her fork around and did some show ponying … only to get tamed by the sexy black cowboy.

We, of course, had left space for Felicia's improvisation style amongst some self-choreographed moves. Felicia, in her horse mask and white spanks, found some white wings before we walked onto the stage. Next minute we had a white Pegasus galloping across the stage in an impressive dance … and I mean, actually galloping … have you seen how long Felicia Foxx's legs are? *DAAAAM!*

Felicia's lovely long legs aside, that was the beautiful thing about working with black queer mob. Our processes are based in our cultural ways. It involves listening to all, leaving space to hear comfort zone needs and styles, and then adapting to conditions. We're storytellers and I see Koori Gras as an amazing platform for our community to step up, explore and have a go. I mean, with biggest mob black, queers community filled with friends, family, Drag

Queens, and all the glitter in the world … what *more* could you want in a family?

Bee Cruse is a Storyteller across roles and mediums, born and bred on Cabrogal country (a clan within the Darug nation), whose family comes from the Gomeroi, Wiradjuri and Monaroo-Yuin peoples of NSW. Bee is the Community Engagement Coordinator for Solid Ground—Blacktown Arts' long-term partnership program with Carriageworks. Bee's stories focus on strong Indigenous culture, people from the urban Liverpool area and Bee's American Indian and Chinese ancestry. Bee has worked in film, theatre and television alongside Rachel Perkins and Wayne Blaire on *Redfern Now* and *Cleverman*, and with Urban Theatre Projects as the Assistant Director of Home Country for Sydney Festival 2017. Bee is a creative with a strong interest in global politics, uses art for social change.

KOORI GRAS 2019
JAMIE JAMES

In February 2019, Carriageworks in association with Moogahlin Performing Arts and Sydney Gay and Lesbian Mardi Gras presented Black Nulla Nightclub. Following a one-week intensive creative development workshop, participants performed their developed works at Black Nulla Club Night alongside popular local and interstate drag artists.

Jamie James recorded the workshops and presentations. Here are some of the images.

OPPOSITE: FELICIA FOXX, BLACK NULLA, KOORI GRAS, CARRIAGEWORKS 2019. JAMIE JAMES

MAD B, BLACK NULLA, KOORI GRAS, CARRIAGEWORKS 2019. JAMIE JAMES

COLIN KINCHELA, BLACK NULLA, KOORI GRAS, CARRIAGEWORKS 2019. JAMIE JAMES

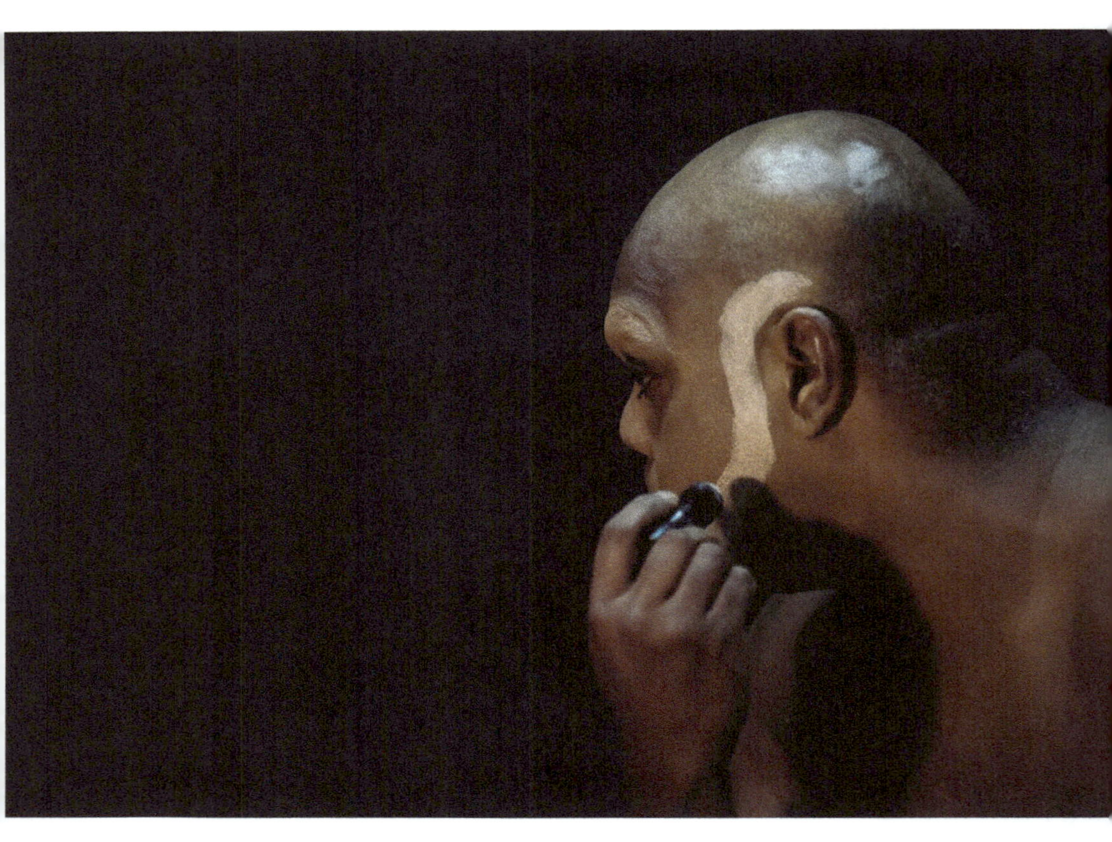

DALLAS WEBSTER IS NOVA GINA, BLACK NULLA, KOORI GRAS,
CARRIAGEWORKS 2019. JAMIE JAMES

BEN GRAETZ, MISS ELLANEOUS, FROM PARTY PASSPORT, KOORI GRAS WORKSHOP, CARRIAGEWORKS 2019. JAMIE JAMES

FELICIA FOXX, BLACK NULLA, KOORI GRAS, CARRIAGEWORKS 2019. JAMIE JAMES

BEE DAZZLED SHANKS—THE PRINCE OF REDFERN (R) AND DADDY COOL, BLACK
NULLA KOORI GRAS, CARRIAGEWORKS 2019. JAMIE JAMES

NANA MISS KOORI, NOVA GINA, SAM BARSAH, BLACK NULLA, KOORI GRAS,
CARRIAGEWORKS 2019. JAMIE JAMES

Jamie James is an Australian photographer. Jamie has been exploring the art form for over three decades, taking a deep interest in various community themes through creative documentation and scene-based engagement. Some of Jamies' works consider community portraiture and in particular, examinations of the cultural shifts in communities' self-representations and performativity.

SINCE COMING OUT
JODIE HARE

I can remember the night I came out to my friends and family like it was yesterday. On hiatus from University because my mental health had been making it impossible to leave my bed, I decided to force myself out for the evening. I have always struggled with mental health problems, but that year I was beginning to crumble internally because I could no longer repress and ignore a part of my identity that I had been conscious of for some time.

Even now I can't explain why I had been so terrified of being honest with my loved ones. I was confident that I was privileged enough to be surrounded by people who wouldn't find my coming out an affront. I knew deep down that any loss I incurred would be a blessing. And yet, this didn't calm my anxieties.

On that cold Tuesday evening, emboldened by enough double vodkas to last me a while, I sent my mum and my friends a text. Ever sophisticated, I didn't divulge too much information and just typed 'I swing both ways, just thought you should know.' As I suspected, I wasn't met with any hostility, just reminders that I am loved in any form I choose to take. My mum's response is one I will always keep close to my heart, 'well fair play to you … lesbitrons still have babies bitch.' As I sat waiting for the train the next morning, slightly hungover and shivering as a light flurry of snow fell all around me, I realised how much lighter I already felt. As if the weights I had been carrying on my back had lessened since my confession. I was almost angry at myself for having waited so long, for denying myself this sense of freedom.

Since that day last year, I have spent a lot of time cultivating what I call my 'gay bubble.' I've pushed myself way past my comfort zone to try and slip inside London's LGBTQ+ community (although I still feel as though I am just on the periphery). I have made friends with other queer women and I have loved and lost someone important for what feels like the first time, though in reality this is not the case. Inside this gay bubble of mine I feel comfy and at ease. I try not to get involved with the arguments about who gate-keeps sexuality, and instead just relish the fact that I get to love a woman if I choose to. Sometimes however, this bubble is popped. Each time I speak to a new doctor, a new colleague or try to make a new friend I am forced to come out all over again. And on these occasions, in conversations with strangers, I do not feel as safe as I did that first time. I am lucky enough that so far, I have not experienced violent or dangerous reactions, but that is not to say that the ones I've had have been pleasant. In these moments, when I have to witness the obvious disgust on people's faces, the subtle shuffle away of the chair, or the patronising, 'now why would a pretty girl like you waste yourself doing that?' I am reminded that outside of my gay bubble, anything that doesn't resemble cisgender heterosexuality still isn't the norm. It's still different. Strange. Not discussed. It reminds me that by creating my gay bubble I have lulled myself into a false sense of security. But do you blame me?

Naively, I assumed that coming out as bisexual would be the end of the inner turmoil I felt with regards to my sexuality. I thought I had found my label and that it would stick. Unfortunately, this year has proven me wrong. After the end of my first relationship with a woman, I took the time to reflect on the ways it differed from those I had had with men. In short, it was better. Much better. I had more fun, I felt more loved and I felt like I didn't have to defend who I was as a person as much. In fairness, this could have been due to the fact that I had chosen a much kinder partner than those I'd had in the past, but I had an inkling that it was something more than that. In that moment I opened up a line of questioning that I struggle with internally on odd days, and every time friends ask if I'm 'just a lesbian now.' I don't know, is the honest answer. I know that even if I am still bisexual, my attraction to women is much stronger than that towards men. But really, that is all I know. I have thought about the relationships I've had with men. Relationships that have been laced with abuse and co-dependency. I remember the gut-wrenching nausea I felt at 15 when all my friends had had boyfriends already and were starting to become suspicious about my lack of interest in the opposite sex. I remember that the first relationship I had was with the first boy who had been interested in me. I wonder now if I had really wanted that relationship or if I coaxed myself into it in a bid to fit in when I had already spent so much time feeling like I didn't. The second relationship I had with a guy came a few months after what was arguably the most traumatic event of my life. I wanted someone to take care of me and protect me, someone who would make me feel safe. Did I actually want it to be a boy, or did I just latch on in desperation to what felt familiar and secure? I can't answer these questions right now, maybe I'll never be able to. Feeling anchored to the label I attach to my sexuality is a balancing act, and I alternate between bisexual and lesbian all the time. A few days ago, I came to the stunning realisation that, in reality, it doesn't bloody matter. I don't need to waste time trying to categorise myself, and I don't owe anyone an explanation of where I fit. All that matters is that I get to sprinkle my love over whoever I want.

54

Jodie Hare is a Postgraduate student currently working towards an MA in Modern Languages, Literature and Culture at King's College London, and hopes to one day work in the publishing industry.

VERA BENNETT—WENTWORTH. MEL SIMPSON

THE WOMYN'S CIRCUS
JEAN TAYLOR

An extract from *What Are Dykes Doing?: Collected Non-Fiction*, by Jean Taylor (Dykebooks, Melbourne, 2019)

I'm standing on my head, fingers intertwined, forearms braced along the floor as I ease my feet away from the wall and balance there for a second or two. Feeling my body stretching upwards, feet pointed towards the ceiling, and aware that, like many of the activities I find myself doing at the Womyn's Circus, I've never done this before. And I'm doing it now.

Me.

Balanced on my head like the circus veteran I'm rapidly becoming.

When I first joined the Womyn's Circus on the 23rd April, 1991, I was a forty-seven year-old lesbian feminist whose motto was: 'whenever I feel like exercise I lie down until the feeling passes'—(Robert M Hutchins). As a political activist the most exercise I got was walking on the IWD, ILD and Reclaim the Night marches, writing the minutes at the various collective meetings and doing a stint at the photocopier from time to time.

So, you can imagine my shock and horror when I went along to those first workshops where I was expected to do handstands, forward rolls, warm-up exercises, including one that was aptly named 'sit-ups from hell', cartwheels, shoulder stands, thigh balances and other contortions too complicated to describe. Then it was climbing ropes, walking along the tightrope, swinging on the trapeze, womyn standing on my shoulders and balancing on my up-stretched legs while I lay on the floor.

It used to take me several days of agony, with aching muscles I never knew I had, to recover from each workshop, in time for the whole process to start all over again. My body, which had never struck anything like it in its life, was stupefied. My mind wasn't coping too well either. Whenever Sally, our trainer, told us what we were going to do next, and always something that I'd never contemplated doing for a minute in my wildest dreams, my head would be muttering, *you've got to be joking! You want me to do what?*

Mind you, we did do some gently co-ordinated poi work. I was also learning to juggle, and just occasionally we did an exercise that,

much to my surprised delight, my body was quite capable of doing.
And, of course, as the weeks went on, everything got that much easier
to do, my body was invigorated rather than agonised and I was
beginning to feel pleased with myself and the skills I was achieving.
By the end of that first year I went into the performance rehearsals as
one of the stilt walkers, albeit on the smallest ones, and more than
capable of doing a few plate tricks, as well.

I'm not a little proud, I don't mind admitting, that I was able to
work through the fears I felt while I was learning to walk on those
stilts. To the extent that, after my experiences during the three week
season of the performance where we were walking on our stilts
outside on the uneven group, nowadays I feel quite confident each
time I strap the stilts to my legs, stand upright on my own and take a
walk around the warehouse space. And have even progressed to
slightly higher stilts already this year. Indeed, my first public
appearance as a circus womyn was when I lead the Reclaim the Night
march in Geelong in October last year and did the entire walk of
several city blocks on stilts. As for the plates, I can toss, drop and
catch them in a way that makes it look co-ordinated and magical in
true circus fashion. I have to say, I can juggle, but it's not what you'd
call a fascinating sight as yet, but every now and then I pick up those
balls and keep working on it.

I stand, legs apart and slightly bent, my arms extended to grasp the
biceps of the womyn either side. And another womyn starts climbing,
one foot on a thigh, the next on my shoulder to stand upright. The
next womyn stands on my thigh on the other side and eventually is
standing with one foot on my other shoulder. And so on. Till we
three standing braced in a triangle as the base have three womyn
standing balanced in a similar fashion on our shoulders and holding
on to each other for support. And Sally is saying that the next step is
to get a womyn standing on the shoulders of the three womyn on top
of us.

My mind fairly boggles at the image this conjures up. I know that
the strain on the face of the womyn next to me to maintain the
balance we have just now achieved is reflected on my own. That the
muscles in our legs and arms are straining to stay braced without
collapsing, that our shoulders will be aching this week because the
feet of these womyn have had to be rearranged to find the correct
spot to stand on our shoulders without undue agony. To even
contemplate a third tier under these circumstances is beyond our

capabilities, let alone begin to imagine how she might possibly get up there in the first place.

And yet, after these many months of placing my body in positions I'd not thought possible, I have come to an appreciation of Sally's indisputable skills as a circus trainer. If Sally says that a womyn will stand on the shoulders of the womyn on my shoulders then quite naturally, somewhere along the line, that will happen. I have learnt that if a womyn stands or sits on my body in a way that her foot fits against my neck by following the contours or her knees are placed on my bent back, just so, then I hardly feel the pressure of her full weight at all. I have learnt that being 48 and physically lethargic is no barrier to developing circus skills and becoming a whole lot fitter than I've been for many a long year. It's also confirmed for me the value of womyn-only workshops, of taking responsibility for ourselves and our learning processes and beginning to trust in our own innate abilities as well as the dexterity of others.

I'm tying up the bootlaces of the pair of roller skates I've just put on my feet for the very first time in my entire life. I stand upright and step onto the concrete floor to try them out. It's like slipping on glass and I clutch frantically at the rail to stop myself falling. I have no balance whatsoever. This is one of those moments when I say to myself, what the fuck am I doing with roller skates on my feet yet, I'm reminded that the first aim of the circus is to have fun. This is fun? Floundering around making a fool of myself? I think back to my very first time on stilts and how petrified and incompetent I'd felt wobbling around and learning to fall on my padded knees so I wouldn't break my wrists. And how far I'd come to be able to call myself a stilt-walker, these days.

A couple of weeks later, I'm roller skating round the large warehouse space, very tentatively, very cautiously, still terrified of falling, but look at me, no hands. And all being well, I might very well, come performance time in October/November this year, be as capable of roller skating as I am now on stilts, miraculous as that may seem now from my very tenuous position, swaying around on these tricky little wheels tied to my uncoordinated and fearfully inexperienced feet.

Jean Taylor is a radical lesbian feminist writer and activist based on Wurundjeri country in Naarm (Melbourne), Australia. Jean's books include *Stroppy Dykes: Radical Lesbian Feminist Activism in Victoria During the 1980s* (2012) and *Lesbians Ignite* set in Victoria during the 1990s. Her work can be found at www.dykebooks.com.

HANNAH BUTTSWORTH

Renascence represents a growing awareness of identity while within a condemning environment and the cathartic experience of celebrating the freedom to be oneself. I focus on LGBT+ individuals who still experience social discrimination despite changes in Australian and international laws that make it possible for them to have easier life experiences. Many young queer individuals still feel uncomfortable and unsafe when coming out. I have used the iconography of religious art throughout my body of work to highlight how the ideals of religious art contradict the reality that causes much of this social rejection.

II. HANNAH BUTTSWORTH

III. HANNAH BUTTSWORTH

INTERVIEW
MAUDE DAVEY

Bent Street publisher Gordon Thompson talks with actor Maude Davey.

I meet with Maude on a late Saturday afternoon in Collingwood—the best available moment as Maude is deep in rehearsals for two upcoming shows—*Anthem* and *Gender Euphoria* at the Melbourne International Arts Festival (October 2019). I remind Maude that the first and last time we actually met was on a short film shoot (*Engaged,* dir. Susan Long) in 1991. I was the cameraperson and Maude and I spent half a day together in the cubicle of a toilet, for her character (in the story) has taken refuge there during a dance party.

Maude: That's right!—Migod, I remember that. And you were standing on the toilet seat!

Gordon: Me and a handycam. I nearly fell in the toilet when you flushed it by accident. It's a little while back now, but—hey—so, what have you been doing these last thirty years? Back then I think you'd been dipping your toe into cabaret?

Maude: Yes, that was all through the Miss Wicked Competition.

Gordon: Tell me a bit about that.

Maude: What happened in the 90s there was this lesbian cabaret, or this queer cabaret scene, and people ran monthly events, or big parties—such as the Docks parties at Shed 14. The ALSO Foundation ran them, there was Red Roar and Winterdaze and The New Year's Eve parties, so there were three big parties every year down at the docks, and then there were little monthly events in small venues on Smith Street, or in North Melbourne, with 100 to 300 people, with shows like She's Famous, or the Ruby Lounge that Amanda Morris ran, and the Caviar Club—a DJ outfit—and they used to run women's parties.

And when we say 'cabaret' cabaret meant a different thing back then. We called it cabaret because we didn't really know what else to call it. And it was queer cabaret. It was basically whatever you wanted

to do—you'd sing a song, or you'd do a weird fetish-based act, or you'd do a circus thing, or some dance, like Amanda was really into the Vegas feel—so, big tits and feathers and stuff. And there was a whole side of it which was driven by the sex-positive movement, like the S&M dykes from Sydney and that was Wicked Women. And that was all about celebrating—you did a night of performance in a pub and at The Club here in Smith Street, and it would all be about a celebration and expression of sexuality.

And then there was ACT-UP, and an organisation called GLAD (Gays and Lesbians Against Discrimination). There were also fundraisers for positive living—those would be big parties—not big, 400 to 500 people, that sort of thing, unlike the docks which were thousands.

Gordon: And you were able to do cabaret performance there?—I'm asking that as my image of cabaret is something small and intimate. The Isherwood / *Cabaret* thing. Did that translate?

Maude: The club performances were different from the smaller rooms. You did different things. The club performances were much more spectacle-based, much more outrageous costumes, more people on stage. Bigger gestures. So you could sing songs, but there was also a lot of lip-syncing and dance routines.

Maude: No, there was the individual performer—there were big stars in that world who came out—Paul Katsis. But certainly, at the Mardi Gras and docklands parties, yes, that was about mass—you'd get four people on aerial acrobatics, eight male and eight female dancers … but the GLAD parties and those kind of things—maybe I'm exaggerating, maybe it was more like audiences of 200, but they felt bigger than a small cabaret room, but they were fundraisers—so you'd want to sell 250 plus tickets, but there'd be a band and you'd get up and do a weird thing.

Gordon: So if we jump cut to now, what have been some of the changes to 'cabaret'?

Maude: One of the things that happened was that there was a resurgence of the thing we now call cabaret, which is that intimate room, people doing all the Eartha Kitt songs, or people doing shows about their journey with an illness, or whatever, and singing songs about that: you know, a girl, a piano and a mike stand. So, that came back in a big way. That's what the Adelaide Cabaret Festival calls cabaret, it concentrates on bringing Kristin Chenoweth over to sing the hits from her Broadway shows. Think of Ute Lemper doing the same kind of thing.

Gordon: And you wouldn't want her not to.

Maude: No! She's bloody good at what she does. But all that wasn't around in the 90s and early 2000s, so we were doing what we called 'cabaret', then 'cabaret' in that form came along, and so we called what we were doing 'burlesque'.

Gordon: Where does that word come from?

Maude: It actually has a verb form—'to lampoon', to satirise. And it has deep historical roots. Burlesque originally was a vaudeville show with a lot of skits and songs, routines that satirized the state of things. It was often sexually risqué and often involved drag. So, come the 2000s queer cabaret turned a corner and became burlesque. The other thing about the 2000s was a movement in performance-making towards very small venues. Suddenly people were doing shows in rooms where 20 people could fit, or two—they were building their own tents. That was the beginning of the Garden of Unearthly Delights, and the village that visits the Fitzroy Gardens every year. And then there was the Spiegeltent.

Gordon: Which set a kind of standard ... well, maybe it did or it didn't, but you feel as if it took things to a new level.

Maude: Well David Bates had brought the first Famous Spiegeltent to Australia and what Spiegeltent did was create a venue that had its own feel, like that club in the film *Cabaret*, like the great clubs, it provided a platform which had feel, which had style, aesthetic.

Gordon: It was, is, a great brand.

Maude: Yes—and David produced *La Clique*, the first big Spiegeltent show that toured all over the world and was very successful and that was variety, but it was, in the early days, very queer. So most of the performers were queer—Ursula Martinez, Le Gateau Cocolat, Frodo Santini (not queer but very weird). Its difference was that it wasn't a titty show; the nudity, the sexual adventurousness was driven by a queer sensibility, rather than by a heteronormative 'girls taking their tops off' to shake their tits at a bunch of heterosexual men getting drunk in the corner.

So there was queer cabaret in the 90s; and then Spiegeltent comes along and there's a movement back to transportable, smaller venues, a more intimate performance style, and *La Clique* was a major show or event in the development of the idea of the Spiegeltent Show as we understand it now, which is variety, which is act, act, act. You put a singer in, you put a circus performer in, an aerialist. But what I'm saying about *La Clique* is that one of the things that made it so special was that it was driven by queer sensibility, rather than what happened to the burlesque movement. We did cabaret in the 90s, then cabaret became a thing which we didn't understand ourselves to be doing and then we called ourselves burlesque, and then that became a thing we didn't understand ourselves to be doing and burlesque became girls with feather boas and corsets shaking their bosoms in a very heteronormative way.

Gordon: So it lost a particular queer and political edge?

Maude: Absolutely. When it becomes mainstream it loses that.

Maude: … Well, burlesque never quite descended to *those* depths. And look, there are some great burlesque artists who do beautiful classic burlesque. There are great things about it. I love what people call neo-burlesque. And it's usually driven by queers, and it's usually in very small bars, and it's not paid well, and it does weird things like women laying eggs on stage, and people like Moira Finucane and Ursula Martinez, Jess Love and Amy Saunders, and Chris Green. And it's in London, Australia and America. People like Julie Atlas-News and Matt Fraser—there's a whole neo-burlesque scene in New York which was really weird and really interesting. And so that was the 2000s into the early 20 teens, then the burlesque thing went a bit downhill. I don't know what 'thing' we're in at the moment—I'll have perspective on it in five years. We're kind of in 'variety' at the moment. People want to do variety. Variety is easier to make than theatre.

Gordon: Just going back to that mainstreaming of burlesque, you did a show—My Life in the Nude—that revisited some of your feelings about that. In a video you said that taking your clothes off for performance had become less comfortable over time?

Maude: I think what I was saying, or exploring there, was that in the 90s I would take my clothes off on queer platforms and that's not uncomfortable; but then as the 2000s progressed and I was working in Moira Finucane's shows—such as *The Burlesque Hour*, which was actually two hours; and *Glory Box*—and the audience changed and the platform became more popular, more mainstream—which is everything that you want it to do—but taking you clothes off in that environment when you're a woman who is in her mid-forties and who is not particularly interested in perpetuating a heteronormative oppressive 'stereotype', then *that* became more and more uncomfortable. And so I made 'My Life in the Nude' as a kind of farewell to that kind of performance, to put it to sleep … and then what I did was, my sister Annie and I decided to find out what kind of variety you can make when you're over fifty.

So we put together an outfit called Retrofuturismus, which was circus and weird performance. And one thing that came out was an interest in how short-form variety format can be more than just 'I'm gonna sing a song', 'I'm going to do a trapeze act' and how it might articulate ideas about the world. And that's an ongoing quest of mine, to figure out how you can appeal to people's intellects as well as their guts, in short-form performance. I love short-form, it's so great … you think in 3 to 4 minute chunks; in theatre—my god—you've got to invest so much attention and time and money and effort to make something that might not work and you're only going to do one season of it anyway; but you make a good three-minute act you can do it over and over again. It has legs, it has life. You can travel it.

Maude: A variety of things. Sometimes, okay, it's a text-based approach: I write lists of things I can do, I write a poem, and you wander that around in your head till you come on to something.

Other pieces are driven by a song that you want to sing, or a track that you want to work to. Other things are driven by a skill you want to perfect, or … you know, weird things. You know, I was at the soccer one day, at my son's soccer game, and I find that deeply, deeply uncomfortable because I'm having to be a soccer mum and talk to the other mums. So I pull out my little book and write this thing, and I'm thinking, 'Don't look at me, don't look at me—I'm a bush, I'm a bird'. And that became an act that I did in a show.

The ideas come from anywhere. And with variety, the simpler the better, because what you want is something that speaks on several levels, or says several things, but in the simplest possible way. If the idea's too complicated it probably won't work. And sometimes you can progress an idea a long way, then put it in front of an audience and find that it's not going to work! It's just not going to work!

One of my big projects is *Gender Euphoria*.

Maude: Yes, and that's a celebration of trans identity.

Maude: Yes. And that came about because I met a cabaret singer called Mama Alto who's a trans woman and she was in one of Moira Finucane's shows. And I heard this thing said that something you can do to make a difference to the world is mentor people who don't look

MAUDE DAVEY, MAMA ALTO, CO CREATORS OF **GENDER EUPHORIA**. ALEXIS DESAULNIERS-LEA

like you. And so, I love Mama's performance, she doesn't need mentoring in terms of her artistry, but I suggested to Mama Alto that we make a show together and this is it. It's my attempt to move out of my comfort zone, move out of working with white ladies—that's the selfish driver, or one of the selfish drivers—but it's fantastic, it's an amazing show.

Gordon: Is it ready to roll, or are you still developing it?

Maude: No, we're still making it. We presented it at a one-off event in January at the Arts Centre and that was a beautiful show, but we want it to be better, and bigger, and we're bringing guests in. We're bringing in an artist Krishna Istha in from America who is a non-binary trans person whose done quite a bit of performance in Melbourne. And we're bringing in a Tiwi Sistergirl, Crystal Love, from

Darwin. So we have guests and we're making more acts. We're ambitious for the show. We want it to travel. We want it to be a platform that can do the circuit and incorporate other performers, that can have a revolving lineup, or be the same show depending on the situation.

Maude: I don't know that. I will say though that we're working with known conventions. We want to make it an audience pleaser. We're not in a small room with a tiny audience doing experimental shit.

When the risks are low with a small audience, that's when you can be experimental. When you're on at the Melbourne Festival—I don't want to give them a show that's so experimental that the Melbourne Festival audience walk out going, 'I didn't like that. Why did they program that?' I want the 'conservative' Melbourne Festival audience who come to this show to walk out saying, 'Wasn't that magnificent!' 'Aren't those artists amazing!' 'Isn't my position on trans identity now shifted somehow'. It's a mainstream audience; you've got to give them things they understand. Particularly because it's a celebration. I don't want to slap them in the face, or challenge them too hard—there are other venues for that, and other avenues for that. I'm all up for that, and have done a lot of that, and will continue to do so. And because there are of course a lot of harmful debates, or discourses, on trans identity going on right now, what we really want to do is create visions of joyous, fulfilled, successful people that you look at and go, 'This is a wonderful person; and isn't this a wonderful artist'.

Maude Davey is a performer, director and writer who has worked at the forefront of contemporary performance in Melbourne for the last thirty years. In the 90s she toured nationally and internationally with her acapella/theatre outfit, Crying In Public Places; in the 00s she toured nationally and internationally with Finucane & Smith's acclaimed *Burlesque Hour / Glory Box* variety show and in the twenty teens she has produced her own variety platform, RetroFuturismus, which has been presented in Melbourne, Sydney (Sydney Festival), Brisbane (Wonderlands Festival) and Darwin (Darwin Festival). She has also been the Artistic Director of companies in Adelaide and Melbourne (Vitalstatistix and Melbourne Workers Theatre), and acted regularly in film and television (Sisters, *Offspring, The Slap, Summer Heights High, My Year Without Sex*).

AYMAN KAAKE

Born in Tripoli, Lebanon, Ayman Kaake travelled to Australia in 2011 to pursue the study of visual arts. A telecommunications engineer and cinematography graduate, he left behind his parents and eleven siblings as he set off on his artistic journey. Applying his creative vision then led to diplomas in photo-imaging and visual arts from Melbourne Polytechnic, winning best conceptual folio with each. www.aymankaake.com

'Unfortunately, we live in a very sad, greedy manipulative world full of anger and blood. And we, as artists, can only use our art to express that anger and make our voice heard. We deserve a better world!'

THE RED BUTTERFLIES, 2016. AYMAN KAAKE

My work is self-portraits, I use my imagination to create a dreamlike world, documenting feelings and emotions, inspired by my move to Australia, stories I've been told, people I have lost, and the confronting themes of refugee-inspired stories, mostly through a community of friends who have travelled by boat to Australia, harbouring dreams of a better life.

OPPOSITE PAGE: OUR CHILDHOOD HOME, 2016. AYMAN KAAKE

A LETTER TO MY CHILDHOOD SELF, 2018, AYMAN KAAKE

A friend (and a Syrian refugee) once told me, 'We are not alive, we are just surviving', and this has always stayed with me.

MELANCHOLIA, 2016. AYMAN KAAKE

The process of putting together the artwork is just as important to the artist as the final result. My dream is to influence people, and to make them believe in themselves. The world can be changed, and we can be inspired by all beauty surrounding us.

At the heart of creativity there should be one underlying question: 'What makes us happy?'

AT HOME IN THIS PLACE
STEVIE LANE

Growing up in regional WA in the nineties wasn't exactly filled with positive queer representation and community. In hindsight, the idea of connecting with other queer people was completely foreign to me. In fact, for a long time I didn't even know what 'queer' meant beyond a slur, I just knew it was something I didn't want to be.

While I grappled with my own sexuality and gender identity through my adolescent years, all I knew were whispers, hearsay and outright discrimination of people who were 'different', regardless of whether they were actually LGBTIQ+ or not. There was a boy in my primary school who was labelled effeminate and precious by the soccer parents who watched from the sidelines at games. He didn't play for long, and his exit from the world of sports went largely unnoticed. It's only in hindsight that I see how problematic the parents' behaviour was. At the time I was just chuffed to be getting more time on the field. When I was 11, my peers started flippantly calling each other 'fags' and 'homos' as a form of offence. Early on in high school, well into the noughties, the insult 'that's so gay' started to rise in popularity, myself not excluded from using this ignorant phrase. And then, later in high school, there was a girl who looked like a boy who people sometimes called 'it'. It's easy to see then why I felt extremely unsafe in expressing who I was, or even exploring it in the slightest, yet I still longed to connect to others like me.

The internet was not readily available when I was growing up (oh the joy of internet dial up), and I didn't have my own computer until I was 18, so my desire for connection turned to the hidden pages of fiction. The town library was somewhere I felt safe. I liked the quiet that filled the aisles and the privacy of the shelves, and still do to this day. My parents would take me to the library often, mostly because it was free, and I would spend hours browsing shelf after shelf. Sometimes my parents would even drop me there while they went off to run errands after school or on a weekend. I could usually be found immersed in a book in the young-adult section. This was partly because I loved the storylines and endeavored to read them all at some point. But secretly, it was also so I could try and find some semblance of anything queer, to make my queer little heart feel at ease. The mere thought of typing the word 'gay' or 'lesbian' into the library's computer search was utterly terrifying, and the idea of outright asking the librarian for any recommendations … the mere thought makes me shudder, even now. And so, through the shelves I trolled.

I still remember the excitement I felt when I found my first queer book, *Rainbow Boys,* by Alex Sanchez. The book series follows three school-aged guys, as they navigate exploring sexuality, gay crushes, gay relationships (otherwise known as relationships!), coming out, and HIV—all things I had been largely sheltered from until this point. I would have been about 12. When I saw the book's spine on the shelf, I didn't want to get too excited by the title, though my heart did skip a beat. While the rainbow largely represents the LGBTIQ+ community, rainbows can also be representative of many other things … I pulled the book from the shelf, held my breath, and turned my head to look behind me, left and right, as casually as I possibly could to make sure no one was watching. I looked at the photo of the three guys on the front, to my eyes nothing overwhelmingly … 'different'. I turned it over and started to read. My hand clenched the book tighter as I realised it was exactly the kind of book I'd been looking for, for such a long time. Though it didn't exactly resemble how I saw myself, and my experiences specifically, it still had a flashing neon sign above it saying, 'these are your people'. I pretended to look at the other books in my hand, as if contemplating which to pick, then quickly slipped it into the pile. I didn't want people to see the cover, in case they recognised it, and I didn't want people to see the back, in case they read the blurb and exposed me, and so in the middle it sat. I held the pile of books, with the spines pressed against me, to hide the title, and went on my way. This book, and the two in the series that followed, were all I had for a long time after that. I think it's safe to say that I borrowed those books many times over. I like to imagine that there are queer librarians everywhere around the world bringing these kinds of books into libraries for the kids who need them most. For isolated kids like me. A belated thank you to whoever this was at my local library, you gave me something to hold onto.

It's experiences like this, and many others of its kind during my childhood and adolescence, that get me thinking of how different my experiences might have played out had I grown up now in 2019. I'll be honest, I'm a little jealous of how much younger queer people generally are when they come out today, albeit a privilege a lot of young people still don't have because of safety. Though, what's done is done, and the past is past, I still dabble in daydreaming about it.

My reality was: The internet, at least as we know it today, was still very much in development. I was sixteen the first time someone came out to me and I officially knew someone who was gay. It was 2007, texts cost 25 cents each so were sent sparingly, and we were talking in codes and metaphors to hide from the reality of the content of our conversation. From that day on I stopped using the word gay as a synonym for bad, because I knew it would hurt someone I love. It would be a further three years before I came out to that friend, and subsequently realised that most of our friendship group was queer, all step-toeing around each other; individual silos.

What I imagine growing up now would be like, is this: I'm 17. The internet, in all its glory, is a place where people can connect to others from all over the world. I watch YouTube videos of Miles Mckenna inspiring people everywhere by being unapologetically trans and queer. I'm reading Ash Hardell's book *The ABCs of LGBT* and learning about the intricacies of language and identity. I'm hearing stories from brotherboys and sistergirls all over the nation and watching the first trans character appear on mainstream Australian TV, played by a trans actor. I'm watching YouTube videos of Hannah Hart just being herself and talking about her day-to-day adventures with her girlfriend. I am following hashtags such as #transisbeautiful and #loveislove on Instagram and attending rallies to advocate for LGBTIQ+ people's right to not be discriminated against based on religious beliefs. I've just paid for my plane tickets to go to Melbourne to watch a range of diverse stories at Melbourne Queer Film Festival. I'm driving down the coast on my P plates singing at the top of my lungs to Troye Sivan. I'm wearing a binder, telling my queer friends in Perth and around the world that I'm queer and non-binary and pursuing medical transition. Though I didn't get to do all of these things at 17, they are all the things that I do now, at 28, and I've never been happier.

You see, queer representation doesn't just exist on a lone dusty shelf in a local town library anymore. Queer community doesn't just exist within a 50km radius of where you live; it's quite literally all around us. We've gone from purely local, to completely global. Even though the internet can be very distracting and invasive at times, it has allowed us to connect to others in ways we were unable to before. When others have questions about coming out, queer dating or gender transition, we help each other and provide answers and insight based on our own lived experiences. When mainstream media fails, which it often does, we tell our own stories. The beauty of being so connected is that, while we shouldn't and don't have to, we can go out and be the representation we wish to see in the world. Being visible and sharing our story is a truly revolutionary act, in and of itself. In a world that tells us there is something wrong with us, that we are going to hell, we can simply be ourselves, speak our truth and prove them wrong. When someone who is scared, isolated and being forced into a mould that does not fit them, a single story can let them know that things will get better, and that there is a way forward. When people see happy and healthy LGBTIQ+ adults living as their true selves, it lets those people know that it is possible. I've had the most in-depth, personal and eye-opening conversations with people I've never met before from half way around the world. And to be honest, I'll probably never meet most of them at all, and that's okay. Regular human contact with others in person is important, but so is connecting with people who are like you. By connecting with people like me online, I built the strength I need to break free from the oppressive society in which I live; in which we all live. It's not just about how we interact with others, but the basic act of interaction with other LGBTIQ+ people that is truly awe-inspiring. Why? Because it is starting waves of liberation around the world and saving lives; it certainly saved mine.

I've been back to where I grew up several times now since leaving at 18 (10 years ago). Each time I go there, I see that it is more inclusive than the last time. I am so happy that there is visible queer representation and community in the little town I used to call home. While I know 'things are a lot better now than they used to be', I know there'll be many people in the town who still struggle with their identity, and there always will be so long as we live in a heteronormative and cisnormative society. That's why I choose to share my experiences as a trans and non-binary queer person, and why I think a lot of people choose to share their experiences. It's because everyone wants to feel connected to others in some way. Everyone wants to have common shared experiences, so they know they aren't alone; so, they can feel at home. And at the end of the day, home is not about a physical space. It's about belonging and acceptance, no matter where you grow up and live in the world—and everyone deserves to have that.

Stevie Lane is a queer filmmaker and writer, raised in Albany and based in Perth, WA. They have a Communications degree and are currently studying a Master of Commerce in Marketing. When not sharing their own experiences, or those of other LGBTIQ+ people, they work in the mental health sector educating others and raising awareness of LGBTIQ+ issues.

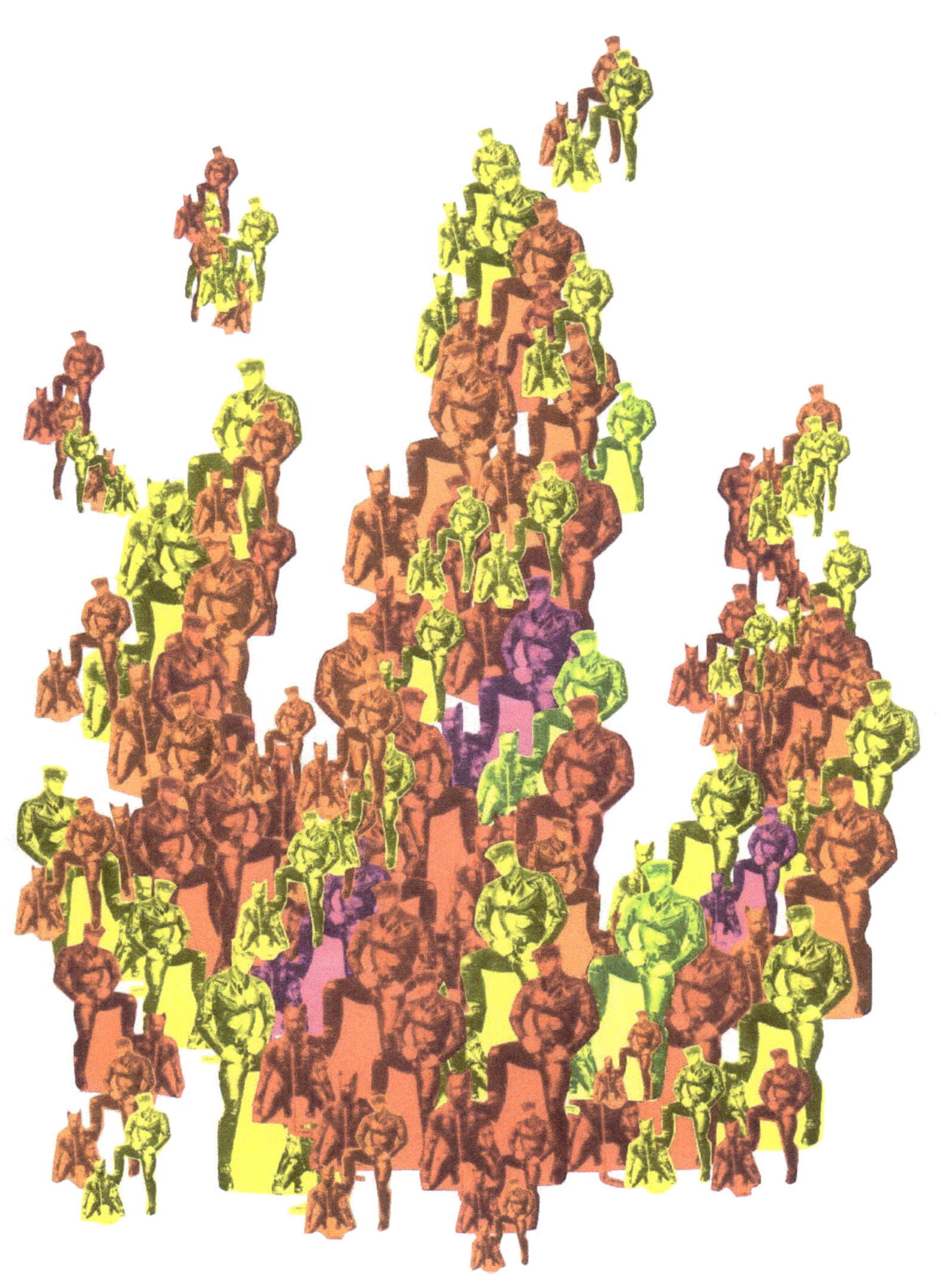

LEATHERMEN COLLAGE. GUY JAMES WHITWORTH

LEATHERMAN-MADE CLIMATE CHANGE
GUY JAMES WHITWORTH

So, and this might be the gayest thing I've ever written, but here goes: isn't collage fabulous!!

And just to confirm that we are on the same creative page here, collage is the cutting out and sticking down of ready-printed images to compose a new image. Oh my, if you have never tried it, please do, what fun!

It's kind of strange that, as someone who spends a lot of time being a professional creative, I would choose another creative project as a hobby, but I like the idea of taking something already in existence (so much easier than starting from scratch) and improving on it!

And call me shallow if you will, but it doesn't harm that collage is rather 'hip with the cool-kids' at the minute. If you search #collage on Instagram, Pinterest or TikTok (OMG, get me, I'm so freakin down with the kids) you'll find endless cool and inspirational stuff.

I co-run a fortnightly drawing group for LGBTQI Elders here in Sydney, and I'm always on the lookout for activities that are both easy and exciting. And, lemme tell you, collage ticks those boxes a treat! Inexpensiveness, readily available materials, instant results and a visual narrative should we choose to introduce one. However, there's a bit of a hurdle to navigate before introducing the attendees of the drawing group to the joyous reveal of my new creative pastime.

Now I hate to be a Debbie-downer-party-pooper here, but unfortunately there is a badly cut out dark cloud that looms over the silver-lined picnic of collage: namely all the future landfill fixtures needed to do it! I know, I know, it's a buzz kill isn't it; environmental concern alert! There's always that one annoying fool at a house party who's in the kitchen whingeing/screaming hysterically about 'don't use the plastic cups, they'll never decompose and they strangle all the turtles', when all you want to do is just pour a gin and tonic and tell them to shut up.

But it's true, plastic cups will NEVER decompose! And this is the thing, likewise, have you ever tried to find resharpenable scissors in the modern word that can be bulk-bought without plastic handles? And don't even get me started on how those little single-use plastic-encased glue sticks aren't refillable and have to be totally replaced after the miniscule blobs of glue inside have been used up!

But you know, although it's difficult, I want to try and do this properly, and not just add to the devastation of our worlds' resources, because if, whilst introducing people to the joys of creativity, in reality, I'm just adding the destruction of our world, then I'm not really doing it right, am I?

Okay, I'm going to be honest, I've kind of lured you into this written piece under false pretences. This piece isn't just about the light-hearted frolicsome joys of collage, but about how we, the LGBTQI population of this planet, are actually perfectly placed to be the ones to save it.

Ain't no doubt about it, whoever steps forward and hands out non-plastic cups at a house party, is going to get derided, rejected and excluded by those other party attendees; but this is our superpower: we, as members of the LGBTQI communities are already completely used to that shit end of the social stick! We've already developed coping mechanisms and thick skin when it comes to being 'that person'. So really, if we aren't going to stand up for what we know is unpopular, but right, who is?

As someone who is vegan and has been 'plant based' (ie veggie or vegan) for my entire adult life, I am very used to the sinking feeling and compromise of beliefs needed to stand in a leather or fetish venue as the only one dressed in home-made vinyl or mock leather corsetry or harness. Fundamentally I love the look of the clichéd, big, Tom of Finland-esque, butch, hairy, leathered up daddy type as much as the next queen (be still my beating arse!). But compassion and consent are also ridiculously important to me, both in my real world and sexual fantasies, and the reality of that is, if you're wearing leather, the animal who's skin you are wearing was never compassionately treated and their consent was certainly never given for the torture they endured so that garment could be made for you.

There is no such thing as 'compassionately farmed' meat or leather. No animal ever wants to die.

Cognitive dissonance, it's a real thing, we all suffer from it. It is when someone doesn't connect one thing with another because of denial, or through not connecting the process to the outcome; it's blocking something out if we don't want to think about it—such as purchasing a wasteful single-use plastic glue-stick that has no other destination than to sit eternally in landfill and still claiming to be an

LEATHERMEN COLLAGE (DETAIL). GUY JAMES WHITWORTH

environmentalist. I'm really trying to stop myself from behaving in certain ways because, once I pause and think about my process, I often realise I can do better. We can all do better. There is always room for improvement and it usually really isn't that difficult.

Okay, back to lovely collage. The piece that accompanies this article is called 'Leatherman-made climate change' and is about how, at our worst, we can all engage cognitive dissonance when we choose to and when it suits us. The visual reference is a flame representing both, the burning of the Brazilian rainforests to make way for land on which to graze cattle and the Greta Thunberg quote, 'Act as if your house is on fire, because it is'. It is a piece about how we as human beings can 'other-ise' other beings to the point where they are nothing to us other than a distant part in a process to further our collection of fetishistic accessories, which, by the way has a name; it is called speciesism. Speciesism allows us to neglectfully objectify animals and reduce them to nothing more than just meat and skin.

Cognitive dissonance is something no one wants to admit to, but we all do it, another example of that, would be, let's say, when somebody refuses to see another person's worth because of their sexuality, I think you get the picture there. We can all do better.

86

LGBTQI people definitely can. Let's cut speciesism out of this picture and discard it.

Years ago in my single-and-ready-to-mingle thirties I made myself a selection of good, quality vinyl harnesses (is that the correct plural for a harness, I have no idea, anyway I made several in different colours) because I wanted to go out to fetish venues and go on the sexy-hairy-daddy-hunt and oh yes madam, those homemade vinyl harnesses (and okay, I'll admit it, matching clutch bags) worked a treat thank you for asking.

I, like you, am a complex human being who often contradicts themselves, learns as I go and I certainly am not perfect. I bought lots of glue-sticks before I thought that silliness through; now I try to use liquid PVA where I can, or I use double sided tape when it all gets a bit too tricky, but it's all still very much a work in progress, and again, I learn as I go and admit (at least to myself) when I'm wrong.

I'm aware there's a few heavy-handed metaphors in this piece, but it all forms a complete picture in the end, kind of. Like I said at the start, I like the idea of taking something already in existence (so much easier than starting from scratch) and improving on it. Collage won't save the world, only we can do that. LGBTQI people and conscious decision making built upon compassion and creative thinking rather than cognitive dissonance and needing to be popular at parties can do that. Also, honestly, what kind of person drinks gin and tonic out of a plastic cup?

Guy James Whitworth grew up in Northumberland, England and moved to Sydney over twenty years ago. He is one of those artists that try to use their powers for good and is as well known for his activism around animal rights and social reform as he is for his vibrant annual exhibitions. His style of rich, opulent portraiture often lends itself to elevating repressed and marginalised members of society using the authority of visual art as a medium to do so. He has won various awards and has been finalist in many of Australia's art prizes. His first book, *Signs of a struggle* has been recently published by Clouds of Magellan Press.

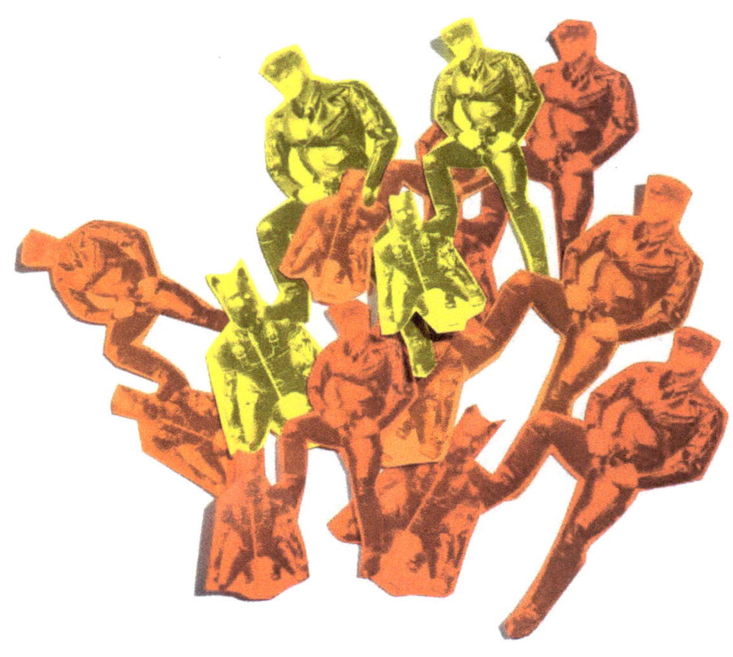

LEATHERMEN COLLAGE (DETAIL). GUY JAMES WHITWORTH

THE DYKEMOBILE
ASHLEIGH HARDCASTLE

I stared at the carpet, hugging a cushion to my stomach. It was heart-shaped, with stumpy little arms sticking out the sides. Kind of creepy, when I thought about it. Usually I chucked it on the ground when I came here; I was too old for cuddle-cushions. I was too old for this place in general, really. Old enough to drive myself here for my appointments, P-Plates blu-tacked to my windscreen. They'd boot me out of the outpatient program in a couple of months, when I turned eighteen. I worried about having to start over at a new place. Did adult eating disorder clinics have cushions with arms, too?

I could feel Jamie's eyes searching my face. She was trying to put the pieces together (tears + silence = ?). That was what they did, these psychs—they tried to read your mind. Problem was, they couldn't, could they? You actually had to talk to them, which sucked. Big time.

I glanced up at her, then looked away quickly. I knew I should say something, but there was a brick in my throat and I didn't have the energy to shift it.

The thing was, I didn't even *want* to talk to her. I wasn't meant to be seeing her today—they were tapering down my therapy sessions and I'd already seen her once this week. I'd only come in to see the dietician, but I'd wound up in here thanks to the flood of tears I'd delivered when I should've been presenting my food journal. The poor dietician had looked completely bewildered. I guess you can't break down the nutritional value of tears.

It wasn't like me to be such a wreck. Public displays of emotion weren't my thing—the way I saw it, tears were best reserved for dark rooms with curtains drawn. But I wasn't myself that morning—I was nursing a hangover and the confirmation of a long-repressed fear. And so the tears had rained the second the dietician asked how I was doing. And once they started, there was no stopping them. They were still falling now, but the tank was running dry and they'd slowed to a quiet drizzle. My skull felt like a balloon about to burst.

'What's going on for you today?'

Jamie had obviously given up on the wait-it-out-and-she'll-talk approach. Her voice made me jump; it was too loud, too sudden. I missed my old psych—she was young and cool, and had nice eyes and a soft voice. But she'd upped and left a few weeks ago, right when I was transitioning from high school to uni and needed her most. It wasn't fair…I'd been spilling my guts to her twice a week for two years, and suddenly I was expected to just carry on with someone new. Like it was that simple. If she'd still been here, then maybe I could talk. *She* wouldn't judge me, I knew that. But Jamie? I couldn't be sure.

Still, I felt bad that I wasn't giving her anything to work with. It wasn't her fault she'd been lumped with me, and she probably had better things to do with her morning than sit here watching my face leak. I mustered up all my energy and swallowed hard, managing to shift the brick in my throat just enough to squeeze a few words past.

'Something happened,' I said, my voice catching at the edges. 'Last night. With my friend, Hannah.'

That was it. That was all I could say. The brick had shifted back up and called for reinforcements. I'd said too much already. My cheeks burned and my eyes dropped lower, no longer seeing carpet. A series of memories flashed through my mind, like the faded slideshow my nanna once showed me.

I picked at the lint on my jumper.

I slink into a bottle-shop with Hannah—the dodgy one down the road from her student accommodation. We choose wine the colour of concentrated urine because it has the highest alcohol content for the lowest cost, and laugh gleefully when we make it out without getting asked for ID…

Pick.

We slurp wine from plastic cups in Hannah's paint-splattered room. The wine makes my face pinch, but the taste improves the more I drink. And so I keep drinking…

Pick. Pick.

We're chatting and laughing and our voices are loud. Hannah's edges are blurred and everything we say is hilarious…

Pick, pick, pick.

Hannah's lips are on mine or mine are on hers I'm not sure which but it feels good. My lips are numb and clumsy…

Pick pick pick pick.

We're fumbling with buttons and my heart is pounding because I know what comes next and I've never done it before and I'm excited and nervous and not sure it's right but somehow it feels inevitable…

I squeezed my eyes shut against the next image, slamming the doors on the memory.

When I opened them again, a fresh stream of tears dampened my cheeks and I shook my head silently in response to Jamie's gaze. I couldn't tell her. I just couldn't.

I went back to analysing the carpet, wondering what Hannah was doing now. When I woke up this morning and realised what had happened, I panicked. What was she going to think? Would she regret what we'd done? Would she be completely grossed out and never want to see me again? Had I ruined one of the only friendships I'd managed to cling onto since leaving school?

Feeling sick with shame and hunger, I'd dressed and slipped out while she was still sleeping, longing for the comfortable sameness of the clinic and not caring that I'd be too early for my dietetics appointment. On the drive to the clinic, my head was a whirlwind of worries. I was in shock—but not, I realised, because it had *happened*—rather, because I had *let* it happen. After all, it hadn't exactly occurred out of nowhere. The signs had been there all along; little sparks catching alight, begging to be noticed. But I hadn't wanted to see them.

Now, as long seconds trudged by, the silence broken only by the obnoxious ticking of Jamie's wall clock, I cast my mind back and gave those sparks the attention I'd starved them of. A dream about holding hands with Hermione, at the age of eleven. An obsession with Mary Poppins' eyes at thirteen. The burning shame in my chest when, at age fourteen, my friend's mum made a passing remark that *lesbians* just weren't normal. A questioning email sent to my own mum at the age of sixteen, and the mess of emotions I felt I was dismissed as being too young to know. The fire in my abdomen when a girl who took me under her wing at boarding school invited me to sleep in her room after a movie night. I'd spent the night in a state of half-sleep—my body pressed hard against the scratchy brick wall and my hands tucked firmly into my armpits—petrified I might accidentally brush her skin with mine.

Each time a spark had ignited, I'd quickly stamped it out and brushed the ashes under the carpet. It was easier to ignore them than to face the prickly questions they raised. Besides, nothing had ever actually *happened*. Not like last night…

Again, I screwed up my eyes against the memory.

'What if I guess what happened?' Jamie suggested, tugging me back to the present. 'If I guess right, will you tell me I've got it?'

I hesitated. Could I do that? Could I admit to her what I did, if she managed to guess? Not seeing a better option, I nodded. She would probably never get it right, anyway. It was too weird.

She smiled. 'Okay, let me see…'

My heart began to race, bouncing erratically against my ribcage. What would she think if she figured it out? That I was disgusting?

Weird? Abnormal? That's what Dad would think, if *he* found out—that I knew for certain. He'd made his views perfectly clear after Mum left him for a woman. From that day, he never spoke her name again, preferring to call her *The Dyke*. He even christened her car *The Dykemobile*, practically spitting the word each time he saw the little red Holden emerge over the hill after my sister and I had spent a weekend at his place. I wanted to ask him not to call it that. I hated the word 'dyke'—it sounded sharp and dirty, coming from his lips. But I stayed silent. He already thought I was too much like Mum.

'Hmm …' Jamie's voice broke into my thoughts. I jiggled my leg, starting to panic. I should have kept my mouth shut. What I'd done wasn't normal. If she guessed right, she'd want to puke.

I pulled the stumpy-armed cushion tight into my stomach. *I* wanted to puke; to expel the messy, knotted feeling in my guts. I mentally revised the contents of my cupboard, listing the foods I could binge on the second I got home.

Jamie leaned forward slightly. 'Okay, first guess,' she said.

I fought the urge to run.

'Did you and Hannah … kill someone and throw their body in a ditch?'

I shook my head quickly, staring wide-eyed at the floor. It wasn't anything *that* terrible!

She took another guess. 'Did you and Hannah … drink each other's blood?'

I shook my head again, the corner of my lips turning up slightly. It wasn't anything *that* weird.

Her tone changed as she made her next guess—the one she'd clearly been leading up to, the one she'd suspected all along. 'Did you and Hannah … make out?' she asked.

A tiny nod.

'Did you have sex?'

I looked up in surprise, my eyes meeting hers. She said it so casually, like she was asking what I had for breakfast (though, in a place like this, that wasn't necessarily a casual question). I examined her face, but there was no sign of horror. I gave another tiny nod.

'So … what's so terrible about that?'

I opened my mouth, but nothing came out.

What *was* so terrible about that? Suddenly I wasn't sure. What had I done wrong, really? I hadn't murdered anyone. I hadn't turned vampire. I'd made out with a girl—a girl I *liked*, a girl I'd been friends with for over two years. We went a little further than I was prepared for, but was that really the end of the world? As I sat across from

Jamie and began to spill words instead of tears, I realised that it wasn't. That, in fact, it might just be the beginning.

When my time with Jamie was up, I wandered across the road towards my little red car—the one Mum handed down to me a few months back. My head was buzzing with possibility and uncertainty; with hopes and questions and doubts. Did I just like girls, or did I like guys too? Had my shame about these feelings fuelled my eating disorder? What were people going to think of me? Were things going to be weird between me and Hannah now?

I didn't have the answers. I wasn't sure what my label was. I had no idea if denying my feelings had caused my issues with food, or if things would improve now I'd acknowledged them. I couldn't predict how others were going to respond when they found out. And I had no idea if Hannah was okay with what had happened, or if she'd want to do it again. The only thing I knew for sure was that, no matter what, there were people out there—people like Jamie—who would take me as I was, whoever that might be.

As I reached the car, my phone vibrated and I hastily retrieved it from my bag. It was a text from Hannah.

'Hey, are you okay? Just wanted to check you're cool with what happened last night? Because I am, for the record.'

A quiet smile cracked the dried salt on my cheeks, and my fingers shook slightly as I typed my response. 'I think I am too.'

I slid behind the wheel of The Dykemobile and started up her engine.

Ashleigh Hardcastle is a Western Australian queer writer and psychologist whose work has appeared in *The Big Issue, Lite Lit One,* and *OUTinPerth*. She has been a fellow at the KSP Writer's Centre and a participant in the CBCA Maurice Saxby Creative Development Program. This story is based on her own lived experience and she is proud to report that she continued driving the Dykemobile until the day it sputtered its last breath.

SAMUEL LUKE BEATTY
IN TRANSIT: SPACE, TIME

In Transit: Space, Time illustrates key moments in Samuel's transition over the past year, how his body has changed, and knowing that he will continue to change over time too. Samuel reflects on reaching certain milestones, such as starting hormone replacement therapy, to then being over a year on testosterone. From having top surgery, to being a year post-op and also having a revision surgery. Each panel illustrates Samuel spending time with his body, taking care of it, documenting it, occupying space in it, and healing in it. So much time was spent waiting for these milestones to happen, yet those moments came and went, and time still goes on. These intimate moments are printed in vibrant blue and fluro pink with Risograph printing.

Samuel Luke Beatty (b. 1995, Sydney, NSW, Australia) is an emerging artist who works with traditional and digital illustration, as well as forms of printmaking and bookbinding zines and artist books. His practice currently uses storytelling and the metaphor of space exploration across graphic narratives to discuss complexities of gender identity in relation to his own experiences as a transgender man. Samuel currently lives and works in Sydney, Australia.

OPPOSITE PAGE: IN TRANSIT: SPACE, TIME (RISOGRAPH). SAMUEL LUKE BEATTY

AS THIS BODY MOVES THROUGH SPACE

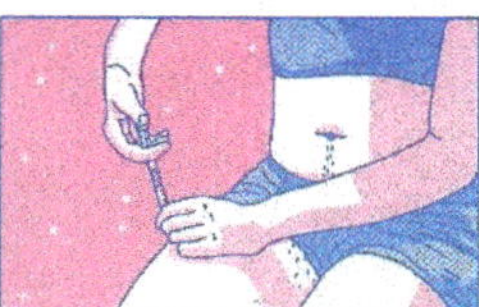

IT SHIFTS AND CHANGES

1 YEAR ON T

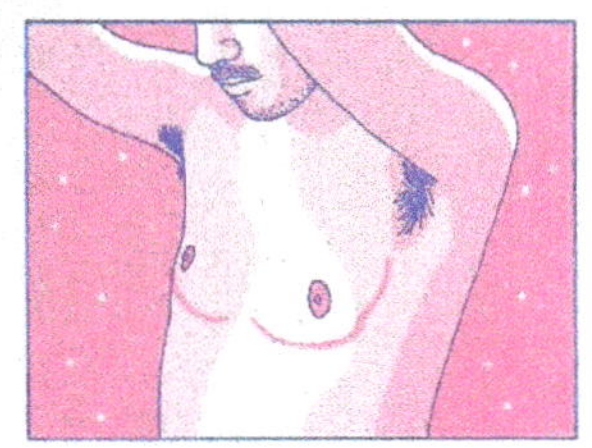

AND I MOVE WITH IT

ILLUMINATING THE REALITY OF MY TRANS BODY

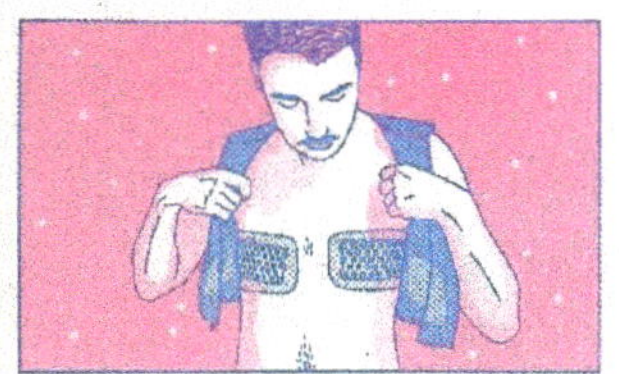

DURING THIS TIME OF HEALING

MY BODY IS A TRANSITIONAL SPACE IN ITSELF

REFLECTING, AND RELEARNING
2 YEAR POST OP
& NIP PORT REVISION

BEFORE IT ALL CHANGES AGAIN

IN TRANSIT: TIME (DETAIL). SAMUEL LUKE BEATTY

ESSAYS

STILL HERE, STILL QUEER, STILL INVISIBLE
MANDY HENNINGHAM

Complications to queer indigenous Australian research

Queer Indigenous people often experiences a conflict in identity between long-standing cultures and new LGBTIQ spaces, particularly brotherboys and sistergirls (Kerry, 2015); however, conflicts are being increasingly challenged as new generations consider decolonising ideas about heteronormativity. In this piece I explore how my queer Indigenous research story also involves conflict around cultural identities, reflecting the wellbeing issues highlighted in current queer Indigenous research and my aims to contribute to the emerging queer Indigenous studies field.

Re/searching for queer indigenous identity

I am forever feeling like I am staring at my own culture through the looking glass. Like I am at a museum. I am both inside and outside of my own culture. This is an experience common to other Indigenous Australians who have had taken or adopted family members (like mine) and have subsequently had shattered community and cultural connections. Not quite knowing where we have come from, with no one to pass on cultural histories, stories and traditions. It has been a decade long journey to find cultural acceptance and understanding.

Whilst my familial cultural connections are fractured, I am involved and accepted in the Indigenous community at the University of Sydney from my time there teaching and studying intersex populations. I have worked as a teaching fellow and an ITAS tutor in the Faculty of Health Science working with a number of Indigenous students of all levels to further their skills in academic development. Through this role, I worked closely with other Indigenous staff at the university. I made myself available for mentoring to students who sought guidance through university. I am a valued and respected part of both the ITAS tutoring team, have built some amazing relationships there with fellow Indigenous staff. Further, I spent most of last year working on a multi-disciplinary project assessing what research is being done with Indigenous Australians, as well as researching and developing strategies for improving Indigenous student recruitment and retention. I have always been very eager to expand my engagement and work in other Australian Indigenous communities.

Towards the end of my final year of my PhD, I began to attend the new Indigenous postgraduate events for students which made me feel truly accepted as an Indigenous woman amongst my peers at the University. Some research has previously highlighted the importance of how building relationships at University is vital to success in higher education for Indigenous Australians (Hill, Winmar & Woods, 2018).

As part of my own cultural journey, I have sought and started to attend cultural classes where I can share my story and learn cultural practices and traditions where I can yarn with other Indigenous people who may have shared a similar history to mine. I have experienced a turbulent journey through my PhD candidature (being required to move faculties and supervisors multiple times). At the same time, I have experienced a difficult time in seeking 'official recognition' as an Indigenous person through my mother's lineage, but these difficulties have built a strong sense of resilience. I use this sense of resilience to push myself further in my career, as well as using it as a building block to mentor other Indigenous students and researchers. Resilience is a strong trait of Indigenous Australians that is required to survive and thrive at university (Hall, Maughan, Wilkes, Thorpe, Forrest & Harrison, 2015). My experiences of colonialism blockading 'official recognition' or even cultural acceptance or access is a shared experience amongst many Indigenous Australians, it feels like everyone has a story. Sharing these stories makes us stronger together and builds our collective resilience as a community.

Re/searching for queer indigenous work

Since the submission of my PhD, I have been seeking full time work. Last year, I was working in an academic position on a project at the University of Sydney to develop a greater understanding of Aboriginal student experiences. I developed an audit of Aboriginal research being done by both Aboriginal and non-Aboriginal researchers with the aim of drawing together a research Network to facilitate networking for staff and students alike who had interest in these areas. This was to create a more collaborative environment in this research space as well as to bring Indigenous academics together. This year, I have been working part-time on some Aboriginal research projects at the

University of Sydney particularly in the ethics application and literature review phases. I have been working on these projects to strengthen my skills in Aboriginal research and to gain experience on working with ethics applications involving the AH&MRC and multiple organisations. This is a way I can give back to my culture and learn from it simultaneously; it allows me to feel accepted in a community and to culturally grow.

Sometimes I experience great acceptance in universities. Other times Indigenous identified university roles have identification proof requirements that are difficult for me to meet, due to a history of adoption in the family. At times, gathering this 'proof' of my identity has been invasive. It can be personally upsetting for myself and my family, as well as being a barrier to gaining work. My skills and experiences in working with marginalised groups like Indigenous and intersex populations do however contribute to my success in attracting work, particularly my experience in working with narratives. Working with narratives to explore the lived experiences of marginalised groups allows for an intimate navigation of experiences that quantitative approaches may not identify. Further, working with mentors who have vast experience in working with transgender and gender diverse populations as well as working with Aboriginal and Torres Strait Islander populations has been key.

I had always known that I would do LGBTIQ research, in one capacity or another. During my Masters degree in sexual health, I became intensely passionate about the medical mistreatment of people with intersex variations and became an advocate and researcher in the area. During my PhD, I worked on some other sexual health projects and began to develop my skills in LGBTIQ research. As an employee, I took it upon myself to become involved in the Ally Network steering committee which advocated for LGBTIQ staff and students on campus. I was never approached for this engagement, I had to seek out these services on campus on my own to see what was being done in the LGBTIQ space; a situation I often find myself in as a 'straight-passing' queer woman.

Conflicting cultural identities

Clark (2014) discussed their own experiences of disclosing sexuality and race; people had asked about them about difficulties of being both queer and Aboriginal or had even questioned that people like us exist. The very questioning of both identities signals the idea that being queer and being Aboriginal are incompatible cultures. Similar to

Clark, I too am met with intrigue at either my race or sexuality, sitting 'on the fence' of both; a pale-skinned Aboriginal woman disconnected from culture and navigating my own living experiences of bi-erasure. Clark's (2014) experiences and my own are subjective but not isolated incidences. There is power in the collection of narratives, and I share my story in this paper to reflect the diversity of experiences had by queer Aboriginal people. Clark (2014) discussed how there are various queer Aboriginal narratives, yet people are often still not listening to them. A blind eye is turned to the multiplicities of culture, lived experiences, and community.

Navigating my queerness is not unlike navigating my cultural journey. My biological makeup and my cis-het relationship status do enable me to retain white and heterosexual privilege which does assist in protecting myself from certain discriminations or unsafe scenarios. However, this socially administered 'safety net' places me on the fringes of both cultures. Many bisexual/pansexual/queer people find themselves excluded from heterosexual groups and biphobic safe queer spaces (Li, Dobinson, Scheim & Ross, 2013) and support groups or experience internalised biphobia (Chard, Finnernan, Sullivan & Stephenson, 2015); never feeling or being accepted as 'queer enough' or feeling like they have something to prove. It is a double-edged sword of both privilege and isolation. In my own experiences, I feel the same about approaching Indigenous cultural events and queer events. I am not 'gay enough' for queer culture and feel too disconnected to be accepted into Indigenous Australian culture. Repeated attempts at building social and work connections require a certain resilience, when outcomes are so uncertain.

Historically, the queer community has struggled to welcome Indigenous voices in Australia, which has also been seen in how queer theory often does not acknowledge the colonial and violent epistemology some queer identities are associated with (Clark, 2014). For example, Clark (2014) discussed commentary surrounding the inclusion of a gay character on Aboriginal television show, 'Redfern Now'. Comments about the character sparked online debates on what is and is not 'real' Aboriginal culture in terms of accepting queerness. Arguments included that Aboriginal culture either ties a person to the savagery and conservatism on one end of the spectrum (barbarism comments including how ancestors would 'have their heads' for it), and 'civilisation' or western acceptance of sexual diversity on the other (that accepting homosexuality is a Western idea, that you 'enjoy being Western'). This highlighted the perceived 'incompatibility' of queer and Aboriginal cultural identities; there is a need for a queer

Aboriginal studies addressing the intersectional experiences and identities of queer Aboriginal people.

Problems for and in research

Existing studies largely group together all Indigenous LGBTIQ people, as it is difficult obtaining enough participants from any single group for quantitative research. There is not data specific only to Indigenous Australian intersex people for example. An Australian study on LGBTIQ youth found 3% were Aboriginal and/or Torres Strait Islander; matching broader population figures for Aboriginal and Torres Strait Islander people (Hillier, Jones, Monagle, Overton, Gahan, Blackman & Mitchell, 2010). It found that the Aboriginal participants were less likely to complete school education and less likely to live in their family homes than the broader LGBTIQ youth population (Hillier, et al. 2010). This highlighted an intersectional barrier to schooling and stability for queer Indigenous youth. Research suggests that bisexual people experience poorer mental health than those who are heterosexual, gay or lesbian (Loi, Lea & Howard, 2017; McNair, Kavanagh, Agius & Tong, 2005; Persson, Pfaus, Ryder, 2015; Taylor, 2019). Bi-erasure and bullying is common in Australian schools (Jones & Hillier, 2016). A Canadian paper suggested a two-spirit antibullying model encompassing a spectrum of queer identities in a fluid, cyclical model rather than a colonial and dichotomous model (Robinson, 2014)—Australian work could consider local options.

Both the trans and gender diverse youth population and the Aboriginal and Torres Strait Islander youth population experience high rates of depression and suicide. Almost half of Australian trans and gender diverse youth have been diagnosed with depression and 38% experienced thoughts of suicide (Smith, Jones, Ward, Dixon, Mitchell, & Hillier 2014). Overall 4% of participants were Aboriginal, Torres Strait Islander or both; a higher population percentage than in the broader population census and a population the researchers emphasised in calls for future research. Research specific to brotherboys and sistergirls is scarce and little is being done to support this group. Sistergirls hold traditional roles such as being medicine people, second mothers to brother-cousins and sister-cousins, and storytellers, yet are often misunderstood in contemporary society (Brown, 2004). A discourse analysis by Kerry (2015) explored research between 1994 and 2012 to explore the differences between Indigenous and non-Indigenous transgender Australians. Kerry (2015) found that Indigenous transgender Australians experienced issues such as difficulty with community engagement, identity, HIV exposure, physical abuse, sexual abuse, and substance abuse (including alcohol). Indigenous transgender Australians additionally experience racism within broader communities as well as in the LBGTI community (Kerry, 2015).

There is a large struggle of identity within this population, particularly as some western definitions of transgender do not apply to brotherboys and sistergirls (Kerry, 2017). A change in identity may result in being rejected by their community and they may be forced to move away from country, however, they are then faced with racism if moving to a larger city. Either of these options can lead to inner conflict and may lead to depression or suicide (Kerry, 2017). An analysis of existing media on Sistergirls found that sistergirls spoke heavily of familial acceptance and rejection, as well as negative responses from community members when discussing their specific roles within community (Kerry, 2018). This reinforces the notion that sistergirls (and brotherboys) face ostracisation from their own communities, where ties to country are vital. Baylis (2015) discussed how the gender and sexual diversity of Aboriginal people is scarcely mentioned in Australian histories which reinforces the heterocentric literature surrounding historic Aboriginal cultures. However, sistergirls in particular have long been a part of communities since before colonisation (Riggs & Toone, 2017). Given the high rates of depression and suicide in the overall trans and gender diverse studies, combined with the high rates of depression and suicide in Aboriginal and Torres Strait Islander population (Fryer, 2019; Korff, 2019), there is a strong need to further explore the needs of brother boys and sistergirls in Australia.

An emerging field from our oldest cultures

Several academics are now pioneering the new field of Indigenous Queer studies drawing on intersections of new Queer ideas with the world's oldest cultures. This is demonstrated via the offering of relevant and progressive units of study including the highly anticipated Macquarie University *ABST1030 Introduction to Indigenous Queer Studies*, the Forum for Indigenous Research Excellence which often holds spaces for Queer Indigenous students and staff such as the symposium on 'Queer Indigeneity in Higher Education'; University of Western Sydney's advertising for academics across the intersection and various community and allied academics studying in

LGBTI research as it intersects with Indigenous identities and
Indigenous studies as it intersects with Queer. It is an exciting time in
research to be contributing to this emerging field for queer and
Indigenous academics across an array of disciplines.

References

Brown, K. (2004). 'Sistergirls'—Stories from Indigenous Australian
Transgender People. *Aboriginal and Islander Health Worker Journal*,
28(6), 25-26. Retrieved from https://search-informit-
com.au.ezproxy1.library.usyd.edu.au/documentSummary;dn=147945
199003273;res=IE LAPA

Baylis, T. (2015). Introduction: Looking in to the mirror. In D. Hodge (Ed.),
*Colouring the rainbow. Black Queer and trans perspectives: Life stories and
essays by first nations people of Australia*, 1–18. Mile End, SA: Wakefield
Press.

Chard, A., Finneran, C., Sullivan, P., & Stephenson, R. (2015). Experiences of
homophobia among gay and bisexual men: results from a cross-
sectional study in seven countries. *Culture, Health & Sexuality*, 17(10),
1–16. https://doi.org/10.1080/13691058.2015.1042917

Clark, M. (2014). Against authenticity CAL-Connections: Queer Indigenous
identities. *Overland*, 215, 230-36. Retrieved from https://search-
informit-
com.au.ezproxy1.library.usyd.edu.au/documentSummary;dn=331795
763420364;res=IE LAPA

Fryer, B. (2019, March 19). Four more Indigenous suicides renew calls for a
national plan. *NITV, SBS*. Retrieved from:
https://www.sbs.com.au/nitv/article/2019/03/18/four-more-
indigenous-suicides-renew-calls-national-plan1

Hill, B., Winmar, G., & Woods, J. (2018). Exploring Transformative Learning
at the Cultural Interface: Insights From Successful Aboriginal
University Students. *The Australian Journal of Indigenous Education*, 1-12.
doi: https://doi.org/10.1017/jie.2018.11

Hillier, L., Jones, T., Monagle, M., Overton, N., Gahan, L., Blackman, J.,
Mitchell, A. (2010). *Writing themselves in 3: The third national study on the
sexual health and wellbeing of same-sex attracted and gender questioning young
people*, Melbourne: Australian Research Centre in Sex, Health and
Society. Retrieved from
https://www.glhv.org.au/sites/default/files/wti3_web_sml.pdf

Jones, T., & Hillier, L. (2012). Sexuality education school policy for Australian
GLBTIQ students. *Sex Education*, 12(4), 437–454. doi:
https://doi.org/10.1080/14681811.2012.677211

Jones, T. & Hillier, L. (2016). The erasure of bisexual students in Australian
education policy and practice. In Pallotta-Chiarolli, M. (ed.) *Bisexuality*

in education: erasure, exclusion and the absence of intersectionality. London: Routledge. pp. 51-71.

Kerry, S. (2014) Sistergirls/Brotherboys: The Status of Indigenous Transgender Australians. *International Journal of Transgenderism*, 15(3-4), 173-186. doi: 10.1080/15532739.2014.995262

Kerry, S. (2018). *Trans Dilemmas: Living in Australia's Remote Areas and in Aboriginal Communities*. London: Routledge. https://doi-org/10.4324/9781315146751

Li, T., Dobinson, C., Scheim, A., & Ross, L. (2013). Unique Issues Bisexual People Face in Intimate Relationships: A Descriptive Exploration of Lived Experience. *Journal of Gay & Lesbian Mental Health*, *17*(1), 21–39. https://doi.org/10.1080/19359705.2012.723607

Loi, B., Lea, T., & Howard, J. (2017). Substance Use, Mental Health, and Service Access among Bisexual Adults in Australia. *Journal of Bisexuality*, 17(4), 400–417. https://doi.org/10.1080/15299716.2017.1401501

Korff, J. (2019). Aboriginal Suicide Rates. *Creative Spirits*. Retrieved from https://www.creativespirits.info/aboriginalculture/people/aboriginal-suicide-rates

McNair, R., Kavanagh, A., Agius, P., & Tong, B. (2005). The mental health status of young adult and mid-life non-heterosexual Australian women. *Australian and New Zealand Journal of Public Health*, 29(3), 265–271. Retrieved from http://search.proquest.com/docview/215705475/

Persson, T., Pfaus, J., & Ryder, A. (2015). Explaining mental health disparities for non-monosexual women: Abuse history and risky sex, or the burdens of non-disclosure? *Social Science & Medicine*, 128, 366–373. https://doi.org/10.1016/j.socscimed.2014.08.038

Riggs, D., Toone, K. (2017). Indigenous Sistergirls' Experiences of Family and Community. *Social Work*. 70(2). 229-240. https://doi.org/10.1080/0312407X.2016.1165267

Robinson, M. (2014) 'A Hope to Lift Both My Spirits': Preventing Bisexual Erasure in Aboriginal Schools, *Journal of Bisexuality*, 14(1), 18-35. doi: 10.1080/15299716.2014.872457

Smith, E., Jones, T., Ward, R., Dixon, J., Mitchell, A., & Hillier, L. (2014). *From Blues to Rainbows: Mental health and wellbeing of gender diverse and transgender young people in Australia*. Melbourne: The Australian Research Centre in Sex, Health, and Society. Retrieved from https://www.beyondblue.org.au/docs/default-source/research-project-files/bw0268-from-blues-to-rainbows-report-final-report.pdf?sfvrsn=2

Taylor, J., Power, J., Smith, E., Rathbone, M. (2019). Bisexual mental health: Findings from the 'Who I Am' study. *Australian Journal of General Practice*, 48(3). Retrieved from https://www1.racgp.org.au/ajgp/2019/march/bisexual-mental-health

THE CHURCH HERSELF
CLARE MONAGLE

On February 24th of this year Pope Francis spoke of the horrific abuse of children that had occurred by members of the clergy, and which had been all too often enabled and then covered up by the leadership of the Catholic Church. He declared *'Brothers and Sisters: in people's justified anger, the Church sees the reflection of the wrath of God, betrayed and insulted by these deceitful consecrated persons'*. At the same time, he insisted that the Church herself remained pure and could ameliorate this crisis. On February 25th, the day after, the news that Cardinal George Pell had been found guilty of child sexual abuse was made public. The timing of these two events was striking. On one day we saw the Pope standing in the Vatican, in the *Sala Regia*, assuming a voice of moral authority, contrition, and yet construing sexual abuse in the Church as a warping of the institution's essentially true and divine mission. The next day we saw one of the most powerful churchmen of his generation found guilty of sexual crimes against minors in a secular court on the other side of the world.

The Pope delivered this statement in the *Sala Regia*, the antechamber to the Sistine Chapel. As he intoned against the evils of the use of children for sexual gratification, the Pope was surrounded by glorious sixteenth-century frescoes that detailed the history of the Church as she triumphed against her enemies. This setting tells us a lot about how the Church understands her mission and her place in history. The Church's task is sacred, divinely authorised from the moment Christ entrusted Peter with the keys to the kingdom of heaven and asked him to manifest his saving work on earth. The Pope is understood to have inherited these keys, as have his predecessors, and have sacred authority to perform God's work in the world. This mission is apostolic, in that it bears an unbroken link with the apostles who served Christ. The frescoes in the *Sala Regia*, which depict Catholic victories, remind the viewer that the Church is always under attack, but that she always prevails because ultimately she is doing work mandated by God.

Always righteous and always persecuted, the Church understands itself to be both all-powerful and yet permanently under siege from those who fail to embrace its authority and its monopoly on the salvation of souls. This mindset seems profoundly hypocritical when considered from outside. The Church proclaims her magnificence across the globe. Her cathedrals declare in stone the permanence of her claims. How is it possible that this institution could understand herself to be vulnerable, to be under attack? The answer is the devil. Because the Church understands herself to contain a perfection granted by God, even if her membership consists of necessarily flawed humans, then any attack upon her is ultimately an attack upon that perfection. And who would presume to attack God himself? Only the devil, that is. To be human is to sin: the idea of our brokenness is at the core of Catholic anthropologies of the person. But we are also made in God's image and so are capable of transcending sin through God's grace (or so goes the theology). The devil, however, has already rejected God wholly and is irredeemable. The Church understands herself to be locked into a cosmic battle for the salvation of these complicated sinful creatures that we call humans, and so, when the Church finds herself under attack the 'logical' assumption is that the incursion is the work of the devil.

If only we were all able to neutralise criticism with such a device. It would be so handy as an explanation. Rather than examining ourselves and contending with our behaviour, we could go on the attack and defend ourselves absolutely. There is no need for soul searching if we imagine our critics to be indelibly evil and destructive. There is no need to think about the implications of our actions if we are entirely confident about our legitimacy and righteousness. This is the psychological theology that informs the Church's response to clerical sexual abuse. There are sinners in the Church, and the sin of sexual abuse is indeed heinous. But the crimes permitted by the clergy need not, and do not, invalidate the Church herself. And as we have seen in the myriad cases of denial and obfuscation of these crimes, at enormous cost to the victims, the response of the Church of the sexual abuse crisis has always prioritised the interests of the Church over those of the children violated by her representatives. The Church herself, you see, is sacred.

I am not explaining any of this to mitigate the Church. In fact, I want to do the opposite. I need to make sense of the Church in order to understand how it has been able to do the profound damage that it has done to those entrusted to her care. I grew up in the Catholic Church. Her rituals and her theologies are in my DNA. In times of sadness and joy, comforting prayers arrive unbidden to my conscious mind. The tragic excoriating beauty of Christ on the cross reminds me, whenever I see a crucifix, of what it is to be broken in an

imperfect world. As a mother, agonised by the depths of my love for
my children, I think of beautiful Pietas that bear witness to the
sublime suffering inherent to the maternal. And as a sexual being a
part of me remains conflicted and anxious about what it means to lust
and be lusted after, in spite of the fact that I have been in a
heterosexual relationship with the same man since I was 19, and I am
46 now. This sounds as absurd to me as it must sound to the reader.
My sexual life has been as hetero-normative as can be, and sanctioned
by marriage (albeit one performed in a registry office rather than a
church). My husband and I have two children, a boy and a girl. We
have a mortgage and a Camry. And yet, from the time I decided that I
would have sex before marriage and that I would really enjoy it, I felt
that I had left the realm of the Church, and sundered myself from the
world in which I was formed.

In good faith, from the time that I became sexually active, I felt
that I could no longer be a Catholic. Before I go on, I should stress
that a great many Catholics do not experience this conflict. Many
members of the Church, probably the majority, who will get married
with a nuptial mass and send their children to Catholic schools, are
relatively unbothered by the Church's teachings on human sexuality.
But speaking for myself, when I, as a young woman experienced the
profundity and rapture of falling in love and lust, and I realised that
the Church sought to deny me that pleasure unless I were to get
married and eschew contraception, I felt I had to walk away. Once sex
and intimacy found me when I met my now husband, which is the
most important event of my life, I realised the punitive violence of the
Church's attitude to sex. The institution sought to disallow the very
experience that was giving me myself. In sexual expression I had
found what felt like the essence of being, to share oneself wholly and
be received with desire, respect and love. I once had a teacher at my
school who described a character in a novel as a '*nasty little tart who
shared herself around*'. What a world, in which the worst thing a woman
could be was someone who shared herself.

So I left the Church as a young woman, but with a heavy heart.
After all, it was my world. Consequently, I have spent my adult life as
a historian of Catholic theology. I am still trying to work it out, and I
miss the Church terribly in spite of myself. But after those two days in
February of this year, I realised that it was over for me. The last time I
went to Mass, to give myself the comfort of the ritual, the priest
reminded the congregation that they ought to be voting no in the
marriage equality plebiscite. How dare they? The actions of the
Church have revealed, in essence, that she considers consenting

sexual relations between unmarried adults (in any gender
combination) to be a greater sin than the sexual abuse of children. So
many of us brought up Catholic have experienced profound
ambivalence about our sexual lives, our harmless sexual lives. We
have been told that the only licit sexual behaviour is that between a
man and a woman whose union has been legitimised through the
sacrament of marriage, and in which the couple are open to offspring
that may result.

Any sexual expression, therefore, that takes place outside Catholic
marriage is a sin. This is what I was told. The only other option is
abstinence. If you hear this enough as a child, the idea will stick at
some level, even if you spend much of your adult life reckoning with
its physical and psychic cruelty. And two or three years ago, I would
have said that it is what it is. While I felt saddened and hurt by this
doctrine in my own life, and the fact that it meant that I felt like I
could no longer be a member of the Church, I felt that I had made
my peace with the loss and was confident in the choices I had made.

But after the Church's response to the plebiscite, and after the Pell
verdict, I am not at peace, I am furious. I am seething with anger at
how the Church has pathologised consenting non-heterosexual
relationships. I am outraged at how many Catholics, of all sexual
orientations, have lost time, joy, pleasure, and love as a result of
internalising this nonsense. And it is nonsense, it has to be. If an
Archbishop can assault boys in his care, in the Cathedral itself, and
still feel entitled to chastise consenting adults about their sexual
choices, then there is nothing good there. The sex is not the problem
here, it is the gaslighting.

The fourth-century theologian Augustine defined evil as the absence
of good. This is the Church now, as I perceive it, she is defined by the
absence of good. The Church has revealed her own profound
emptiness in her acts of abuse, the enabling of paedophile priests, and
the callous refusal to compensate victims and account for these
betrayals. These are all terrible sins. But they are all symptoms of a
larger breach, one that hurts all believers. The Church is enamoured
of her righteousness, in love with her mission, devoted to her
foundation story, so much so that she permits herself the most
appalling hypocrisies. In the past, when I have felt some of this anger,
I have remarked to myself, 'Well, at least we have the Sistine Chapel'.
I love that room. This is the room in which the Pope is elected. In
this room, Michelangelo's extraordinary frescoes take us from
Genesis to Judgement, they bring to life ideas of Christian

anthropology and history with an awesome plasticity that feels divinely-inspired. 'At least we have the Sistine Chapel'. But it is not worth it. The Sistine Chapel is not worth the lives of those children, exploited and broken by a Church that pretended to care for them. And it is not worth the sexual shame engendered by its doctrines, which is felt in the bodies and the minds of so many of us.

Clare Monagle is a strong ally of the LGBTIQ+ community, and a graduate of Monash and the Johns Hopkins Universities, receiving her PhD in 2007. Between 2007 and 2014, Clare worked at Monash University. She came to Macquarie University at the end of 2014 and is an Associate Professor in Medieval History. She is broadly interested in history of intellectuals in the Middle Ages, as well as the histories of the institutions that housed them. More particularly, she is currently engaged with the uses of gendered categories in scholastic thought between 1150 and 1520. Her work is also concerned with the 'medievalism' of twentieth and twenty-first century thought, that is, the uses to which the concept of the medieval is put within definitions of modernity and progress.

GREETING CARD 2: ASHLEY SIEVWRIGHT

ENDING LGBT CONVERSION PRACTICES
TIMOTHY W JONES, JENNIFER POWER & TIFFANY M JONES

Why law reform is not enough

At the opening of the 2019 Victorian Pride March, Victorian Premier Daniel Andrews announced that his government would be the first in Australia to *introduce new legislation to ensure so-called 'conversion therapy' is against the law—once and for all*. Victoria joins over 20 jurisdictions around the world that have legislated or commenced legislative processes to limit or ban conversion practices targeting lesbian, gay, bisexual or transgender (LGBT) people. The Victorian announcement followed the publication of our pilot study report and a report by the Victorian Health Complaints Commissioner, which demonstrated that LGBT conversion therapy remains a significant problem in Australia (Jones et al, 2018; Jones, 2019; HCC, 2019). Yet, as is starting to be realised, legislation alone is limited in its capacity to end harmful LGBT conversion practices. Other, more challenging, interventions are also required.

What are conversion practices?

Conversion practices are grounded in the conviction that all people are born with the potential to develop—properly—into heterosexuals, with a gender identity that accords with the one assigned to them at birth. It views LGBT people as suffering from 'sexual brokenness', which is often attributed to childhood trauma, sin, or treated as an addiction. Advocates of conversion practices seek to 'cure' LGBT people or assist them to be celibate and suppress their gender and sexuality. Full membership and participation in faith communities can depend on LGBT people of faith committing to chastity and seeking 'healing' for their sexual brokenness (SOCE Survivor Statement, 2018). Religion-based conversion practices have not included forced medical interventions on people born with intersex variations.

Harmful 'intersex conversion therapies' need to be addressed in their own right.

Though the term 'gay conversion therapy' is often used in media representations both in Australia and abroad, Australian self-advocates have chosen to refer to LGBT (or LGBTQA+) conversion practices. This is because formal therapy performed on gay men is only a small part of the broader set of conversion practices. These practices often occur in informal or secretive settings and regularly affect lesbian, bisexual+, and trans people. Psychological research has demonstrated conclusively that attempts to 'heal' LGBT people do not reorient their sexuality or gender identity and may, in fact, lead to long-lasting harms (What We Know Project, 2017). We estimate that 10% of LGBT Australians are currently vulnerable to LGBT conversion practices by being members of religious communities that promote conversion ideology and practices (Jones *et al*, 2018). In 2018, banning LGBT conversion 'therapy' was identified as LGBT Australians' top priority (Karp, 2018).

Do conversion practices happen in Australia?

Religion-based LGBT conversion therapy has been practised in Australia for at least the last fifty years. At the same time as Australian psychiatric authorities were declassifying homosexuality as mental illness in 1973 and ceasing attempts to 'cure' it, conservative religious organisations in Australia were developing their own spiritual and counselling practices directed toward the sexual and gender reorientation of LGBT people. Over time, Australian LGBT conversion movements became affiliated with a global network of similar religious LGBT conversion organisations.

The range of LGBT conversion practices that emerged in the early 1970s, in what was then known as the 'ex-gay movement', have changed little over the past fifty years. They are an eclectic blend of popular self-help practices, behavioural and psychoanalytic therapies, and spiritual activities. These involve: twelve-step, Alcoholics Anonymous-style accountability groups (one was literally called Homosexuals Anonymous); individual, group, and online counselling; residential camps; testimonial and self-help literature and videos; exercises aimed at developing 'normative' gendered behaviour; prayer, spiritual deliverance and spiritual healing. Around 7% of Australian LGBTIQ+ students are currently exposed to related practices and messaging through schools (Jones, 2015).

Why is conversion attempted?

Behind these practices sits a curious and contradictory blend of ideologies that seek to explain the aetiology of LGBT and gender diverse identification, and hence how to reorient them. Heavily influential is the 1950s psychoanalytic view that trauma in childhood can disrupt normal psychosexual development. Therapeutic analysis—group or individual—is thus deployed to identify these traumatic events, enable the traumas to be healed and psychosexual development to be repaired (hence this approach is sometimes called reparative therapy). This psychoanalytic approach is combined incongruously with behavioural psychological approaches, which understand human sexuality and gender identity as homologous, and functionally equate identity with behaviour. Practicing and learning to perform heteronormative binary gender and sexual behaviour is believed to equate to sexual and gender reorientation. Alongside these contradictory ideologies of gender and sexuality, are religious beliefs that LGBT identification can be caused by malign spiritual interference. Deliverance from these spiritual forces, including through seemingly benign pastoral care and peer-based support groups, is believed also to lead to sexual and gender reorientation, or healing.

At the beginning of the conversion therapy movement, practitioners expressed a high degree of confidence that motivated and faithful participants could achieve reorientation. In recent years, perhaps mindful of increased external scrutiny or in genuine acknowledgement that reorientation is rarely, if ever, achieved, proponents of the ex-gay and ex-trans movement have moved away from this confidence. At least in public statements, religious bodies and conversion organisations increasingly promote chastity and celibacy for LGBT believers and say that participants should not expect their identity to change. They nonetheless hold out the possibility of change, adding that nothing is impossible for God.

At the core of all these practices and ideologies, including the recent incarnations promoting celibacy, is the assertion that LGBT desires and identities are a form of psychological and spiritual brokenness. These beliefs enshrine deep contradictions and conflicts in LGBT believers. To be a member of a religious community that is not affirming of your LGBT status, is to be saturated in messaging that you are inherently and inescapably broken and sinful to your core.

Are conversion practices harmful?

Most of the psychological studies of formal LGBT conversion therapy to date have focussed on the efficacy of attempts to reorient people (APA Task Force on Appropriate Therapeutic Responses to Sexual Orientation, 2009). While all reputable studies have shown that reorientation is not effective, few studies have documented the harmful impacts of theses attempts to shift gender or sexual identity (Turban et al, 2019). In our pilot study, the harms reported by our participants were profound. All participants had experienced severe mental health difficulties, including suicidal ideation, as they struggled to integrate their sexual, gender and religious identities. Participants reported experiencing difficulty forming relationships and difficulties with sexual function following their experiences with conversion practices. Participants experienced feelings of guilt at the trauma they put others through, including other LGBT people they encouraged to engage in conversion activities. Those who had married a partner of the opposite sex in attempts to achieve reorientation expressed deep sorrow at the hurt and conflicts this led to. Many of them were estranged from members of their families. Other studies also showed young Australians exposed to conversion messages were considerably more likely to think about self-harm (81.8%), enact self-harm (61.8%), think about suicide (83.6%), and attempt suicide (29.1%) (Jones, 2019).

One of the least reported but most profound harms experienced by survivors of conversion therapy was moral injury, or spiritual harm. Many participants resolved their identity conflict by leaving their community of faith. They expressed deep sorrow at the loss of faith, community, and belonging that this entailed. Those who retained their faith lived with a continual tension, experiencing varying degrees of rejection from both their LGBT and their religious communities.

What should be done about this?

It is clear that conversion practices violate international human rights law in several aspects including the right to health for LGBT people, the right to non-discrimination, and the convention on the rights of the child. Conversion practices may also constitute torture, or cruel, inhuman and degrading treatment. In the light of their human rights obligations, numerous jurisdictions around the world have passed laws banning LGBT conversion therapy (Drescher *et al*, 2016). Most commonly, this has involved passing legislation forbidding health care professionals from conducting conversion therapy with minors. In 2016, Malta passed the most extensive legislation so far, which bans conversion therapy being practiced with minors or vulnerable people by any person, makes it unlawful for a professional to offer or perform conversion practices, criminalises referral to conversion therapy and prohibits conversion practices from being advertised.

Our pilot study report recommended that Australian jurisdictions pass laws similar those in place in Malta, but recommended civil rather than criminal penalties be imposed, for reasons which will be unpacked below. This recommendation was adopted by the federal ALP, who revised their policy platform to include provisions to make conversion practices unlawful and support communities to improve their care of LGBT people (HRLC, 2018). Our recommendation, and the ALP policy change, were not widely understood. The Australian Christian Lobby interpreted the ALP's shift as stating that conversion practices should be lawful, and cited it as a victory for conservative religion. Some members of the LGBT community, perhaps viewing the recommendation and policy through the ACL statement, were outraged that broad criminal penalties were not proposed.

At a time when the sexual sins of the churches are more in public view than ever before, there is significant public appetite for the churches to be called to account. The Royal Commission into Institutional Responses to Child Sexual Abuse exposed long histories of grave sexual offences being covered up, denied or minimised. Religious opposition to marriage equality was bare faced, and often brutal (Eades & Vivienne, 2018). In this context, it is not surprising that there is outrage at the harmful practices and teachings of the LGBT conversion movement: they deny the dignity and humanity of LGBT people, including LGBT people of faith. And it is not surprising that the apparently moderate position of making such actions unlawful, but not criminal, needs explanation.

Why make practices 'unlawful, but not criminal'?

There is a fine, but significant, distinction between 'unlawful' and 'criminal'. Unlawful conduct is prohibited by law, but not necessarily at the more serious or higher level of a criminal offence. The practical difference is that unlawful acts are pursued by the victim, seeking a personal remedy, such as financial compensation. Criminal acts are pursued by the police in order to punish the perpetrator on behalf of the state.

There are a number of reasons why it may be better to *make many LGBT conversion practices unlawful, rather than criminal offences*. Broad based criminalisation of conversion practices could potentially criminalise the victims of these practices. Most adult recipients of conversion practices have sought those practices out. If the acts that they sought were made criminal, they would potentially be accomplices in a criminal offence to which they are also victim. Similarly, many conversion practices involve peer activities, where the victims of conversion practices and teachings are effectively perpetrating on each other. Because civil law is focussed on remedy for victims, rather than punishing crimes it allows for an appropriately nuanced application. It also has a lower burden of proof that the victim is required to meet.

A range of criminal and civil penalties have been imposed in the conversion therapy bans that have so far been passed around the world. But recent research is showing that these are largely ineffectual. A recent study of conversion practices in the US showed that of the nearly 80,000 minors that will undergo conversion therapy there, only 25% of them will see a licensed health practitioner subject to the laws currently in place (Mallory et al, 2018). The vast majority of people subjected to conversion practices will experience them in religious settings, where the bans do not apply. And in many jurisdictions, even licensed mental health practitioners are exempted from conversion therapy bans if they affirm that their conversion practices are religious, and not connected to their professional license. New York City recently announced that it would be rescinding its ban on LGBT conversion therapy to avoid legal challenges that could end up protecting LGBT conversion therapy (Mays, 2019). While we welcome the law reforms proposed in Australia, the problem is so complex that law reform alone will not be enough to end it.

In conclusion ...

We know that attempts to reorient the gender and sexuality of LGBT people are futile and harmful. While law reforms banning these practices have some use, they have so far had limited impact on conversion practices. Most existing law reforms have not applied to the majority of conversion practices. And none of them have, or could, address the toxic environments that saturate LGBT people of faith in messages that they are inherently and inescapably broken and sinful to their core. This is why law reform is not enough. The law can ban some, but not all, conversion practices. However, it cannot ban the ideas behind those practices. To address these toxic ideas, the more difficult work of social and cultural change is required.

This cultural work requires us to peer behind the rhetoric of the culture wars, which masks the complexities of LGBT spiritual health behind a false opposition between the LGBT community and communities of faith. This false culture war binary has left many LGBT people bruised and spiritually wounded, and many religious communities fearful, and feeling under siege. Yet when we look beyond the culture wars rhetoric, we see that many LGBT people are religious, and all religious communities have LGBT members. Tragically, a majority of Australia religious leaders (63%) feel ill equipped to provide pastoral care related to gender and sexuality, more than any other issue (AIFC, 2017). What is needed, then, is not just to ban harmful conversion practices, but to educate our communities about how to provide spiritual care to LGBT people that nourishes and affirms them. For, as the psalmist said, we are all 'fearfully and wonderfully made'.

References

Australian Institute of Family Counselling [AIFC](2017). 'Get Equipped: Responding to the growing mental health needs in our churches and communities'. Australian Institute of Family Counselling Report.

APA Task Force on Appropriate Therapeutic Responses to Sexual Orientation. (2009). Report of the Task Force on Appropriate Therapeutic Responses to Sexual Orientation. Retrieved from Washington, DC:

Drescher, J., Schwartz, A., Casoy, F. et al (2016) 'The Growing Regulation of Conversion Therapy'. *Journal of Medical Regulation* 102(2): 7-12.

Eades, Q, & Vivienne, S. eds. (2018) *Going Postal: More than 'Yes' or 'No'.* Melbourne: Brow Books.

HRLC (2018). 'ALP's 'conversion therapy' platform provides better outcomes for survivors. *Human Rights Law Centre News.* December 18. Retrieved from: https://www.hrlc.org.au/news/2018/12/18/alps-conversion-therapy-platform-provides-better-outcomes-for-survivors

Jones, T.M. (2015). *Policy and Gay, Lesbian, Bisexual, Transgender and Intersex Students.* Cham, Heidelberg, New York, Dordrecht and London: Springer.

Jones, T.M. (2019). *Voices of Experience: A student-centred sociology of Australian education.* Dordrecht: Springer.

Jones, T.W., Brown, A., Carnie, L., Fletcher, G., & Leonard, W. (2018). *Preventing Harm, Promoting Justice: Responding to LGBT conversion therapy in Australia.* Melbourne: HRLC & GLHV.

Karp, P. (2018). 'Gay conversion therapy ban found to be LGBTIQ Australians' top priority'. *Guardian.* 4 August. https://www.theguardian.com/world/2018/aug/04/gay-conversion-therapy-ban-found-to-be-lgbtiq-australians-toppriority [accessed 3 December 2018].

Mays, J. (2019). 'New York City Is Ending a Ban on Gay Conversion Therapy. Here's Why.' *New York Times.* Accessed on 12.9.19. Retrieved from: https://www.nytimes.com/2019/09/12/nyregion/conversion-therapy-ban-nyc.html

Mallory, C., Brown, T. & Conron, K. (2019). 'Conversion Therapy and LGBT Youth'. The Williams Institute: UCLA School of Law. January 2018. Accessed on 1.9.19. Retrieved from: https://williamsinstitute.law.ucla.edu/wp-content/uploads/Conversion-Therapy-LGBT-Youth-Jan-2018.pdf

SOCE Survivor Statement. Written by survivors of Sexual Orientation Change Efforts and the Gay Conversion movement. (2019) http://socesurvivors.com.au/

Turban, J., Beckwith, N., & Risner S. et al. (2019). Association Between Recalled Exposure to Gender Identity Conversion Efforts and Psychological Distress and Suicide Attempts Among Transgender Adults. *JAMA Psychiatry.* Accessed on 9.9.19. Retrieved from: doi:10.1001/jamapsychiatry.2019.2285.

What We Know Project (2017). 'What does the scholarly research say about whether conversion therapy can alter sexual orientation without causing harm?' Ithaca: Center for the Study of Inequality, Cornell University. https://whatweknow.inequality.cornell.edu/ [accessed 20 June 2018].

Dr Timothy W. Jones is a cultural historian and Senior Lecturer in History at La Trobe University. Timothy's research interests encompass the intersections of gender, sexuality and religion in modernity. His PhD was published as *Sexual Politics in the Church of England, 1857-1957* (Oxford University Press, 2013). He was lead author of the La Trobe University and Human Rights Law Centre report, *Preventing Harm, Promoting Justice: Responding to LGBT Conversion Therapy in Australia* (2018).

Dr Jennifer Power is a public health sociologist who specialises in research on sexual health, sexuality and wellbeing. In particular, her research has focused on wellbeing and quality of life among vulnerable communities including people living with HIV and LGBT families. She is currently lead CI on the HIV Futures study, a major national survey of people living with HIV, funded by the Australian Department of Health.

Associate Professor Tiffany M. Jones is a sociologist who researches and publishes on LGBTIQ+ issues in education, education policy, health and social policy. She was awarded an ARC DECRA to study the influence of global polity on gender and sexuality on a range of regional contexts and laws (DE160101047). She has undertaken consultancies with: UN bodies collecting data on gender and sexuality in bullying; with the Victorian Government on decision-making for intersex infants; and currently CIHR funded project on reforming health industry responses to intersex youth across Canada, Belgium and the UK.

RAINBOW WARRIORS UNITE!
ALISON THORNE

How historic revolutionaries build resistance today

1960s gay liberationists

Earlier this month I went to see the exhibition *Revolutions, Records and Rebels: Five years that shook the world* at the Melbourne Museum. It focuses on the late 1960s, a period described as *a moment when youth culture drove optimistic idealism, motivating people to come together and question the establishment across every area of society.* The exhibition includes the Stonewall riots, which inspired the formation of the Gay Liberation Front in New York. From the east coast of the U.S. new demands and a vision for complete emancipation soon rippled across large parts of the world, including here in Australia.

These were heady times. In the U.S. the civil rights movement was making waves. Anti-imperialist sentiment was sweeping the globe as colonies fought for their independence. Anti-war sentiment was seething—especially amongst young people—who not only opposed the war in Vietnam, they sympathised with the Communist aspirations of the Vietcong. Workers were striking. In 1968 Paris was in revolt. Early environmentalists, such as Rachel Carson, laid the foundations for eco-socialism. Women were asserting their independence and demanding equality. Is it any wonder that what we now refer to as the LGBTIQA+ community got swept up in the mood of revolt?

The story of the riots, precipitated by a routine police raid on the Stonewall Inn, has become iconic, right down to the parking meter ripped from its foundation and used as a battering ram. The grungy New York bar catered to a camp clientele—amongst them young working class queers from Harlem. Many, including butch lesbians and trans women, rebelled against the gender binary. A significant number of the patrons were people of colour—especially Puerto

Ricans, African Americans and Latinas/os. The bar was an oasis where people could relax and be themselves, even though it was run by the mafia, the drinks were watered down and overpriced, and the threat of police harassment was ever present. While there is debate amongst historians and participants about why *this* police raid on 28 June 1969 sparked a militant reaction, it was a product of the times. The cops raided, patrons rebelled and, as we now know, some of those in the lead were trans women of colour, including Sylvia Rivera and Marsha P Johnson.

Stonewall is well known, but this was not the first time LGBTIQ people fought back. Three years earlier, the transgender patrons at Compton's Cafeteria, a restaurant in the Tenderloin district of San Francisco, resisted police harassment and rioted on the streets. Also less known is some of the history of homosexuals organising *before* Stonewall. The exhibition I enjoyed at the museum includes material produced by pioneering organisations, such as the Daughter of Bilitis (DOB) and the Mattachine Society—both cautiously appealing for acceptance. One famous pre-Stonewall protest took place outside the White House. Part of the strategy was to be just like everyone else: the men wore neat suits and ties, and the lesbians wore smart dresses with stockings and heels. The goals of this 1965 rally were to the repeal of anti-gay laws, declassification of homosexuality as a mental disorder, and equal treatment for gay federal employees.

Those who formed and joined Mattachine and DOB were brave trailblazers, and it would be wrong to pit the pre-Stonewall movement against the flowering of resistance that followed. Many of those who paved the way, doing what was possible in the shadow of McCarthyism, were the *same* people on the front lines of gay liberation a few years later. Gay communist and unionist, Harry Hay, founded the Mattachine society in Los Angeles in 1950. He went on to become an important leader in gay liberation, inspiring the Radical Faeries, a group of gay men who resisted masculine gender roles.

The events that occurred 50 years ago did not create a movement from nowhere. Instead, Stonewall changed the *character* of the movement. Post Stonewall gay lib junked assimilationist aspirations. Emboldened by the politics of the era, the movement evolved to become out, proud and flagrantly different. Gay lib had a different analysis and adopted different tactics. There was an explosion of political ideas in the late sixties and through the seventies, and this led to a movement that embraced the anti-establishment politics of the time with its vision of freedom, equality and talk of revolution. Gay lib made a special contribution with its celebration of sexuality alongside the questioning of gender roles, monogamy and the institution of the family. To get an appreciation of the times, I highly recommend the collection *Smash the Church, Smash the State: The Early Years of Gay Liberation*, edited by Tommi Avicolli Mecca (2009).

1970s socialist feminists

I got involved in the struggle a decade after Stonewall and benefited from early programmatic works by Marxist feminists in the movement, including members of Radical Women and the Freedom Socialist Party. While some queers were happy to come out, embrace the lifestyle of the early seventies, to party and dream of liberation, the more serious in *all* the movements, including gay lib, wanted to nut out how a better world could be achieved. For gay lib, the key to this was getting to the roots of homosexual oppression. Why were gay men, lesbians and *everyone* who challenged compulsory heterosexuality or didn't conform to the strict gender binary reviled? Why was there a price for coming out of the closet? What was the source of homophobia and transphobia?

Key to socialist feminism is the understanding that society has not always been patriarchal, and women have not always been oppressed. The earliest societies, prior to the rise of private property, were matriarchal and communal. As a society developed the capacity to produce beyond its immediate survival needs (a surplus), social divisions emerged, and the technology was in men's hands. All this led to what Fredrick Engels called the world historical defeat of women. Instead of being respected equals in the public sphere, women became enslaved in the private world of the male-headed family.

The twin part of this theory is that the pre-private property societies were not only matriarchal: sexuality was free and there was not a rigid gender binary. A great deal of meticulous research has unearthed important examples, which prove transgender people existed in these societies. Evidence of this can be found amongst First Nations people everywhere, including Asia, the Pacific, Native American tribes such as the Navajo and the people of the Tiwi Islands.

The *Radical Women Manifesto* provides a pithy encapsulation of how matriarchy was overthrown by patriarchy:

> To Marx and Engels, styles in family and sexual relations are varied, historical and transitory rather than biological, cultural or psychological absolutes. The form of the family is

determined ultimately by economics and by property relationships. The family changes accordingly throughout history as social systems replace each other (Radical Women, 2001, p. 22).

The key reason LGBTIQA+ people are oppressed today is that queer lives are a direct threat to compulsory heterosexuality and the sanctity of the patriarchal monogamous nuclear family, which is a key institution of capitalism. While sexism, homophobia and transphobia are policed in different ways, they all have the same source—the rise of private property. Achieving lasting liberation for LGBTIQA+ people means permanently eradicating the source of oppression—the capitalist system, built upon the pillars of sexism, racism, homophobia and transphobia. Gay lib in the late 60s and 70s was a product of the times, and large swathes of the movement embraced anti-capitalist ideas. There was widespread belief that a new world was possible. But by the late 70s, this was subsiding.

1980s queer capitalists

The primary reason was that the economy started to nosedive, and the ruling class wanted to put a lid on rising revolutionary expectations. By the 80s, the world economy was mired in recession and plagued by double-digit inflation and deficit spending. A combination of tactics—both carrot and stick—was used. The stick was state infiltration, harassment and spying. This was particularly the case in the U.S. but there's also evidence of state snooping and manipulation in Australia. Let us not forget the role played by U.S. imperialism in the ousting of the Whitlam government elected in 1972: The militancy of the mass movements in the 1960s and early 1970s had forced the ruling class to deliver significant reforms. Whitlam's ousting in 1975 was the beginning of the take-back.

By way of inducements, capitalism did deliver some reforms, which created space for queer capitalists to set up shop. Plus, small funding grants were offered to movement groups, which started a process of NGOisation—the taming of movements through financial dependency. For example, in the early 80s, gay liberationists in Melbourne received some funding to assist with the publishing of *OutRage* magazine. Set up to cater for the diverse queer community, the publication eventually abandoned radical journalism for pink dollar politics, and its audience became affluent gay men. Although all oppressed people were in motion in the 1960s and 70s and movements influenced each other, most remained single-issue. The Red Letter Press pamphlet, *A Workers Guide to 20th Century,* described the problem this way:

> … while the direct blows delivered by the system were staggering, the movement of the '60s and '70s suffered other fatal weaknesses: internal divisions caused by racism, sexism and homophobia; the lack of politically healthy, mass-based socialist parties capable of providing a revolutionary program and leadership; and isolation from the labour movement, where all parts of the working class are brought together and can effectively express their power (Cornish, 2000, p. 1).

1990s+ queer visibility & marriage equality movements

Despite the changed character of the movement birthed by Stonewall, the LGBTIQA+ community always retained a radical edge, because the importance of coming out and being open about sexuality and gender identity did not go away. The community influenced every corner of society as gay men, lesbians, transgender people and queers of every stripe insisted on being visible and demanded respect. This strategy was crucial, because almost everyone had a friend, family member or workmate who was LGBT. People enjoy music performed by queers, watch TV shows and movies with LGBT characters. Michael Kirby, an openly gay man, had a distinguished career as a High Court judge. The ALP leader in the Senate, Penny Wong, is a lesbian of colour. And, with the Women's World Cup in the international spotlight, and Australia going a little soccer mad, Matildas captain and open lesbian Sam Kerr, is the hero of the day.

The immediate post-Stonewall generation, with its in-ya-face rejection of the monogamy and critique of marriage and the family, would not have recognised the aspirations of the marriage equality movement. On the surface, demanding to be part of an oppressive, patriarchal institution hardly seemed daring. But those, like Radical Women, who dug deeper concluded that elements of this fight had radical potential. Reforms such as no-fault divorce and women entering the workforce *en masse* were already starting to weaken marriage. Based on inheritance and extracting women's free labour, the institution's vice-like grip is slowly loosening. Winning same-sex marriage equality would build on this trend. Radical Women played a leading role in this decade-long fight, co-organising and speaking at the earliest rallies to protest the Howard government's same-sex marriage ban. We intervened with our Marxist feminist analysis, calling out the sexist and oppressive role of the family while explaining how winning marriage rights for queers would help transform this institution into its opposite.

Winning marriage equality was a huge fight and an important victory, but it came at a price. On the positive side, many who are not themselves LGBTIQA+ joined the fight. But unfortunately, over time the fight for marriage equality lost its edginess when it became single-issue. Shorn of any kind of radical analysis, many drawn into the fight now think the battle has been won; they've folded up their rainbow flags and headed home. Despite recent welcome global gains, such as winning marriage equality in Taiwan and the decriminalisation of sex between same-sex couples in Botswana, the liberation demanded by the post-Stonewall movement is as far as ever from being won, including in Australia.

Contemporary intersectionality & the resurgent Right

Focusing movement energy on the single demand for marriage equality for so many years rendered many issues crucial to LGBTIQA+ people invisible. Those in the community who are young, Indigenous, refugees, homeless, with disability, immigrant, poor, people of colour, incarcerated, living in remote or regional Australia or with a mental illness have been left behind. Queer issues intersect with every other struggle—homophobia and transphobia exacerbate the struggle. A high portion of LGBTIQ youth are homeless (Hillier et al., 2010). In the post marriage equality landscape, the transgender community in Australia—especially transgender youth—have increasingly become targets. This is reflected in the demonisation of the Safe Schools Coalition.

Homophobic and transphobic violence is on the rise globally. In Brazil, violence against the LGBTIQ community has reached staggering proportions. Marielle Franco, a Black bisexual socialist feminist politician from the favelas, was killed in what is widely seen to be a political murder. The country is an extremely dangerous place to be trans. In the 12 months prior to Bolsonaro taking office, 167 trans people were murdered in Brazil (McCoy, 2019). In the U.S. LGBTIQ people are more likely to be the targets of hate crimes than any other community—now more targeted than African Americans, Muslims and Jews (Park & Mykhyalyshyn, 2016).

U.S. research, produced by the Southern Poverty Law Center, has found that as queers make gains, the homophobes and transphobes are becoming more violent in their opposition (https://www.splcenter.org/). The National Coalition of Anti-Violence Programs in the U.S. collects data about LGBT murders. They found that in the four-year period from 2012 to 2015, the clear majority of those murdered were Black or Hispanic transgender women—the same group that played such a pivotal role at the Stonewall Inn 50 years ago (National Coalition of Anti-Violence Programs, 2018). A separate report by the Human Rights Campaign found that in 2018, 26 transgender people were murdered in the U.S. the majority Black trans women (Human Rights Campaign, 2019). This year, five Black trans women have been murdered, including two recent killings in Dallas. Transgender women of colour are facing an epidemic of violence as racism, sexism and transphobia intersect. Here in Australia, it was this intersection that led to the death in custody of Aboriginal sistagirl, Veronica Baxter, who was denied access to her hormone treatment in the New South Wales prison system.

Trans women of colour played such a critical role at Stonewall, but clearly life today is damn tough for this segment of the LGBTIQ community. In fact, as late capitalism unravels, life is pretty damn tough for *all* LGBTIQ folks who are not rich, white, male, able-bodied and cisgendered. And let's face it, that it pretty much all of us! Things might be OK for gay airline executive Alan Joyce, who heads Qantas. But for the young LGBTIQ call centre workers in the Australian Services Union, who lost their jobs when Qantas moved them offshore to cut wages, things are not so good. Life might be grand for Jason Grenfell Gardner, a gay CEO who works in global pharmaceuticals. But it is far from terrific for poor people living in parts of the world without any form of drug subsidies, who contract HIV because they cannot afford the $2,000 a month charged by price-gouging, big pharma for the life-saving drug PrEP. Or then there is the success story of Trevor Burgess, the first openly gay CEO of a bank on the New York Stock Exchange. I am sure things don't look nearly as upbeat for the transgender woman eking out a living as a sex worker who, despite having an accounting qualification, has been unemployed for years, having been turned down for job after job.

It is true that the movement has made some fantastic gains over the last 50 years through the efforts of tenacious organising by millions of queers globally, but the benefits of these gains are far from evenly distributed. And even when we do win gains, it is necessary to fight to hang onto them. It only takes a cursory glance at the post-marriage equality landscape in Australia to make the point. The postal survey was imposed on the community by the right wing, on its terms, with the goal of defeating demands for marriage equality. Winning the popular vote so strongly was a victory for LGBTIQ people. This was ultimately the result of half a century of organising. But having won this reform, the fight now will be to keep it. The right wing is not going away. Their latest tactic is organising to entrench so-called religious freedom. This demand is little more than a call to green-light the right to discriminate.

Making common cause

As the global economic crisis worsens, we are living in an ever-more polarised world with the far right gaining increasing influence in many countries. Fascists and neo-Nazis are seeking to build movements, supported by their parliamentary enablers. To do this, they need scapegoats to distract people from the real source of their misery. The LGBTIQ community is right up there, joined by a range of other targets—foreigners, the unpatriotic, immigrants, Muslims, Jews, single mothers, people on welfare, the unemployed, First Nations, refugees, urban elites, greenies, political correctness, halal food, fake news, socialists and anarchists. The targets may vary, but the end goal of fascism is to remove all democratic rights, crush the trade unions and the ability of the working class to resist.

While 21st century fascists may present in slightly different ways, we have really seen this all before, and we must learn the lessons from history. Long before Stonewall and Harry Hay founding Mattachine, Dr Magnus Hirschfeld formed the Scientific Humanitarian Committee in 1897 in Germany—the first homosexual rights organisation anywhere in the world (Dickinson, 2014). Hirschfeld and his colleagues organised for three decades, making important inroads. This era saw the rise of a vibrant and visible gay and lesbian community in Berlin during the Weimar Republic. This was all swept away when Hitler and his Nazis came to power and homosexuals, alongside of Jews, Roma, people with disabilities, Slavic people, non-Europeans, Communists, Jehovah's Witnesses, Catholic clergy, Soviet citizens and Spanish Civil War refugees were all systematically murdered.

In the current polarised environment, we must be ready to defend every gain won by the LGBTIQ movement over the last 50 years. We can certainly see how reforms can be rolled back by looking at the current precarious state of abortion rights, which are being steadily eroded in the U.S. The most crucial steps for the LGBTIQ community now are to make common cause with everyone the far right seeks to target. We urgently need to unify with a common goal to stand together against the bigots and fascist bully boys to stop them *now*. We need a broad and democratic united front to mobilise in massive numbers, ready for collective self-defence every time they seek to organise. We need to drown out their toxic message and stop them from growing and cohering a mass movement. We can't afford to be disunited or to dismiss the threat. And we certainly can't rely on the capitalist state to do the job for us. Right here in Melbourne, Radical Women has direct experience with being part of protests where police frustrate anti-fascists while openly assisting neo-Nazis to parade through the city wearing swastika insignia. Just this month, neo-Nazis crashed the Pride March in Detroit. The film footage of police facilitating the Nazis' provocative march through the Pride parade should be a wake-up call for anyone who thinks the police are somehow on our side.

Sylvia Rivera and Marsha P Johnson and all who rebelled for three nights on the streets of New York in June 1969 knew that the police are not our saviour. The LGBTIQ community of Auckland, which recognised that Maori and Pacifika members of the community would not feel safe or welcome at Pride while uniformed police were marching, understand this. The LGBTIQ community in Moscow, which faces police repression and laws that make it illegal to hold a Pride March will sure as hell appreciate this. The team from Melbourne's much-loved Hares & Hyenas bookshop working to physically and mentally recover from a mistaken police raid earlier this year will surely understand this, too!

Reflecting for the future

The 50th anniversary of Stonewall is an important time for the LGBTIQ community and all who support queer liberation to stop, pause, reflect and strategise about what next. One person who has done this is Edmund White, who was part of the Stonewall Riots. He wrote earlier this month in *The Guardian,* as a middle-class white 29-year-old who'd been in therapy for years trying to go straight, 'I was initially disturbed by seeing all these black and brown people resisting the police, of all things' (White, 2019). He remembers, when someone shouted, 'Gay is good' in imitation of 'Black is beautiful'; 'we all laughed; at that moment, we went from seeing ourselves as a mental illness to thinking we were a minority' (White, 2019). This really encapsulates the essence of Stonewall—it changed consciousness and raised expectations. White remembers, 'I felt exhilarated by the expression of the indignation I'd repressed for so long. I was joining in, despite my years of submission' (White, 2019). And join in he did! He describes the times, no one wanted to imitate straight life; the community were against 'assimilation'. He still lives in New York and the title of his piece, White men were the first to benefit from gay liberation but it can't end there, gets to the nub of the question. He concludes,

> The first group to benefit from the freedom won 50 years ago were white men; now the struggle continues among young lesbians, people of color, the trans population—and all those living under dangerously rightwing, hostile religious regimes. In a sense this return to gender fluid people and gay and lesbian people of color is a recapitulation of the original Stonewall warriors, those drag queens and tough kids from Harlem. They have given new life to a movement that in big-city America at least has become dull, uninspired and materialistic (White, 2019, p. 1).

We're seeing the same trend that White noted from his New York vantage point happening here in Australia. The movement is being re-energised and it is the most oppressed injecting the new leadership and vision. It really is time for Rainbow Warriors to unite. It is time to unite, to take stock of the challenges and to build serious organisation from the diffuse community and broad radical milieu. We're living in tough times with immense potential and real risks. **Serious** Rainbow Warriors should seek to forge united front resistance to take on the right, build their own leadership and look to join organisations with a proven track record and political program, such as Radical Women.

References

Cornish, M. (2000). 'A Worker's Guide to the 20th Century'. *Freedom Socialist Party, 2000*(1). Retrieved from https://www.redletterpress.org/redreaders.html#guide

Dickinson, E. (2014). 'Homosexual Rights'. In E. Dickinson (Ed.), *Sex, Freedom and Power in Imperial Germany, 1880-1914* (pp. 152-176). London: Cambridge University Press.

Hillier, L., Jones, T., Monagle, M., Overton, N., Gahan, L., Blackman, J., & Mitchell, A. (2010). *Writing Themselves In 3: The Third National Study on the Sexual Health and Wellbeing of Same-sex Attracted and Gender Questioning Young People*. Retrieved from Melbourne: http://www.latrobe.edu.au/ssay/assets/downloads/wti3_web_sml.pdf

Human Rights Campaign. (2019). 'Violence Against the Transgender Community in 2019'. Retrieved from https://www.hrc.org/resources/violence-against-the-transgender-community-in-2019

McCoy, T. (2019). 'Anyone could be a threat': In Bolsonaro's Brazil, LGBT people take personal defense into their own hands. *The Washington Post,*. Retrieved from https://www.washingtonpost.com/world/the_americas/anyone-could-be-a-threat-in-bolsonaros-brazil-lgbt-people-are-taking-personal-defense-into-their-own-hands/2019/07/21/5aaa7578-a716-11e9-a3a6-ab670962db05_story.html?noredirect=on

Mecca, T. A. (2009). *Smash the Church, Smash the State: The Early Years of Gay Liberation*. San Francisco: City Lights Books.

National Coalition of Anti-Violence Programs. (2018). Lesbian, Gay, Bisexual, Transgender, and HIV-Affected Hate and Intimate Partner Violence in 2017. Retrieved from http://avp.org/wp-content/uploads/2019/01/NCAVP-HV-IPV-2017-report.pdf.

Park, H., & Mykhyalyshyn, I. (2016). 'LGBT People Are More Likely to Be Targets of Hate Crimes Than Any Other Minority Group'. *New York Times,*. Retrieved from https://www.nytimes.com/interactive/2016/06/16/us/hate-crimes-against-lgbt.html

Radical Women. (2001). *Radical Women Manifesto*. Santa Monica: Red Letter Press.

White, E. (2019). 'White men were first to benefit from gay liberation—but it can't end there', *The Guardian,*. Retrieved from https://www.theguardian.com/lifeandstyle/commentisfree/2019/jun/19/white-men-were-first-to-benefit-from-gay-liberation-but-it-cant-end-there

Alison Thorne is a founding member of the Melbourne chapter of Radical Women, which hosted this talk at a discussion on 29 June 2019 in honour of the 50th anniversary of the Stonewall Riots. Thorne is a veteran LGBTIQ liberationist and a union delegate. She represents the Freedom Socialist Party in PUSH: Organising and educating for a united front against fascism. Check out Radical Women on www.radicalwomen.org or Facebook Radical.Women.Australia, or contact Radical Women at radicalwomen@optusnet.com.au

PROUD 2 PLAY
LGBT+ inclusion in Australian sport
RYAN STORR

Introduction: counting down the days

Proud 2 Play seeks to promote participation and engagement in sport for LGBT+ youth. My aim is to share some of the work we have been doing at Proud 2 Play, and to highlight some of the ongoing challenges, but also opportunities to increase engagement in sport and exercise for LGBT+ youth. When we first started Proud 2 Play we spent a considerable amount of time engaging the LGBT+ community, and in particular LGBT+ youth. We wanted to hear exactly what young people's experiences in sport and exercise were like, and how we might be able to help them become active, or if they were active, to ensure their experiences were positive and free from discrimination. We knew some key things before we started in terms of what the research told us:

- Many LGB people (73%) do not perceive sporting environments as welcoming for LGBT youth (Denison and Kitchen, 2015).
- Sport and PE are sites whereby LGBT+ youth experience homophobia, biphobia and transphobia (Symons et al., 2010).
- The impact of homophobic bullying in PE has a significant detrimental impact on the mental health of young people, who report higher scores for depression and anxiety (Symons et al., 2014).
- There are no participation rate figures in Australia for LGBT+ youth in sport, but research from the US and Canada (only on sexuality) indicates lesbian, gay and bisexual youth team sport participation is almost half that of heterosexual youth (CDCP, 2016; 2018; Doull et al., 2018).
- We know that when LGBT+ youth are supported by their families, in schools, and by friends and peers, they can flourish and this support can lead to positive outcomes (Smith et al., 2014; Hillier et al., 2010).

The reality of this evidence base really hit home when we spoke to young people and their families about their experiences of sport.

One story stays with me and I often speak about it in presentations. We worked with Head Space and some of their queer support groups, and one day we did a focus group with some young people. It was a mixture of trans, gender diverse, and queer people. Their experiences of bullying in PE and sport were difficult to hear. One young trans person explained that they had written down a countdown in their diary until the day that compulsory PE was over, so much was the extent to which they had been bullied by their peers in a class which is supposed to be fun and enjoyable. Others shared stories of physical abuse, and were often targeted in contact sports.

Others were not allowed to do certain sports; one young boy loved to play netball and do dance, but these were 'girls' sports and therefore he could not play these sports. Another damning story involved a young trans girl around the age of ten, who had socially affirmed their gender identity. Although active and engaged in a range of sports prior to her transition, she didn't think she could do sports as a girl because 'girls didn't do sports'. How a young girl is conditioned to think they cannot do sports, or even if a girl does do sport they might turn into a lesbian, continues to baffle me. In this respect, it is important to understand that the experiences and challenges for lesbian women, gay men, bisexual people, and trans people play out very differently, and their experiences are unique. Take for example, research by Lynn Hiller (2005) which demonstrates that sport, specifically Australian Rules Football, can actually provide a safe space and sense of belonging for lesbian women and girls. In the next section I discuss and outline the case study of Proud 2 Play.

Case study: Proud 2 Play

Proud 2 Play was started and co-founded by James Lolicato and myself in Melbourne, Australia in 2016. We started it at a time when there were significant concerns in the wider LGBT+ population in Australia; the Safe Schools program had come under attack, the marriage equality campaign was gaining momentum (and the No Campaign), and the atrocities at Pulse nightclub in Florida had left many in the community feeling scared and vulnerable. The sport sector too had not always been supportive, and stories of homophobia, biphobia and transphobia (HBT) were common within sport. There was a grassroots movement in community sport too around AFL, spearheaded by Jason Ball, and his inaugural Pride Cup in Yarra Glen. At the time I was doing my PhD which was linked to an Australian Research Council (ARC) grant, which explored how community sports clubs were responding to and dealing with diversity, with a specific focus on cultural, gender, and disability diversity. One of the biggest things to stand out to me as I worked in the Victorian sporting sector was the silence around LGBT+ diversity, or discussions around HBT.

After a closer analysis, there were no specific programs or organisations which specifically aimed to get more young people from LGBT+ communities into sport or exercise (or physical activity, active recreation, leisure etc). Note that Proud 2 Play is an LGBTI+ plus organisation, but within this short essay I mainly use LGBT+ where discussing a specific focus on sexual orientation and gender identity. It is important to not conflate gender identity with sex characteristics, but often the sport sector does. Secondly, I refer to communities, rather than one single community and one homogenous group of people under the LGBT+ umbrella. Under the LGBT+ umbrella there are a diverse range of people and communities. For example, within the gay community there are bear and leather communities, demonstrating that there is a range of identities within communities, and their experiences are diverse and cannot be homogenised.

Due to the lack of programs and policies to promote LGBT+ inclusion especially at the grassroots level, Proud 2 Play was started. We had a simple aim: to increase participation and engagement in sport for LGBTI+ youth. We work with the premise that youth represents under 25, although now our work covers adults too. However, our focus and priority will always be around young people under 25. This is so that young people have positive and meaningful experiences in sport and exercise during their youth, which increases the likelihood of engagement in later life, and that they can develop healthy habits and positive relationships with sport and exercise. Many conversations with adults around our work lead to them sharing negative stories of PE and sport in their youth, which had turned them off sport, especially team sports. Whether that was PE teachers or peers bullying them, picking them last, or experiencing physical assault. We also get many heterosexual allies speaking of negative stories, whereby their sexuality was questioned or ridiculed if they did not adhere to strict stereotypes around masculinity and femininity.

Proud 2 Play has developed and grown substantially over the past several years, and we now have a more refined mission and vision. We started with a mission and vision centred around the need for all young LGBTI+ people to have access to safe and welcoming sporting environments, and although this is still a focus, we have refined it within the context of our strategic plan. Our new problem statement, vision and mission:

> The Problem—LGBTI+ people are disengaged from sport and recreation, as these environments have not kept up with societal change.
> Our Vision—A world where all LGBTI+ people are leading healthy and active lifestyles.
> Our Mission—To ensure all LGBTI+ people feel confident to lead healthy and active lifestyles, in welcoming and inclusive environments.

Our work is varied and diverse, but central is the provision of assistance and support to LGBTI+ communities in helping them become engaged in sport and exercise. This could be getting people physically active and playing sport, or engaging through feeling safe to attend an AFL match, or working in sport, or volunteering and coaching. Some of our work includes:

- Working with families and trans children to find them safe and inclusive sporting clubs.
- Working with a sports club or organisation to develop inclusive policies and practices which welcome and affirm LGBTI+ people.
- Working with a young trans woman who has been denied access to a women's only gym, to find a suitable gym.
- Helping a lesbian or gay athlete who has experienced homophobia whilst playing sport.
- Partnering with a local council who wish to increase participation in their locality for LGBTI+ residents.
- Working with sports to host inclusive come and try sessions, to attract new people to their sports.
- Helping young trans and gender diverse people try a number of sports and activities in inclusive spaces, to help address mental health concerns.
- Liaising and partnering with schools to ensure equal access and participation for trans and gender diverse young people.
- Providing education to sports organisations, State Sport Associations and National Sports Organisations around LGBTI+ inclusion.

Most people engage in sport and exercise as a form of leisure, for the social benefits, and for enjoyment. If LGBTI+ people wish to do so in the same way but it is not fun and a space they do not feel like they can be themselves or are subjected to abuse, then the core principles of sport are lost.

Cricket Victoria: leading the way

Cricket Victoria was one of the first organisations we began working with, after my PhD research explored how community cricket clubs were engaging with diversity policies and practices. I also worked on several projects as a research assistant, specifically in cricket. We partnered with Cricket Victoria to help them expand their LGBTI+ portfolio, under Cricket Australia's national diversity policy, 'A Sport for All'. Our journey together started when we pitched and applied for funding through Vic Health (A health promotion organisation in Victoria) and their 'Innovation Sport Challenge'. This funding round gave SSO's the opportunity to apply for funding through innovative and social sport-based programs to get inactive Victorian's active, through participation in sport and exercise.

We designed the program based around education and participation. Key features of the program included:

1. Proud 2 Play would design and deliver education to cricket clubs in Victoria, teaching them how to run an inclusive cricket program.
2. Cricket Clubs would attend education sessions and be given help and resources to run a four-week inclusive cricket program (to cater for LGBTI+ young people in particular).
3. Participating cricket clubs would deliver a four-week inclusive program, engaging LGBTI+ participants in their local areas (as well as their friends and families) to come and try cricket for the first time.
4. Those LGBTI+ people who wanted to keep playing or enjoyed their experiences, had a pathway into a cricket club that they know was safe and welcoming.

One of the most important lessons from this work was that unless there is a specific pathway or inclusive program to invite LGBTI+ people into sport, they are very unlikely to go and join a club of their own accord. So many LGBTI+ people have had negative experiences and hold the perception that sporting environments are unsafe and unwelcoming. Unless we show them an alternative and that sport can be enjoyable and not-gendered, they will not engage or play; this is extremely important for the trans and gender diverse community in particular.

Most sports are binary and based around single sex competitions and opportunities. At Proud 2 Play all of our social programs and opportunities to participate, are done on an inclusive basis—all genders, all sexualities, anyone can come and play. This specifically caters for non-binary people or gender nonconforming people, where sport is incredibly challenging; on most occasions there is nowhere for them to play due to binary categories of sport. So for example, in netball or basketball, people play in teams of people, rather than gender.

There is an inherent assumption that male and female bodies are different and that men are superior and overall better at sports. This is not true. Especially at the grassroots level, there are many women who could outperform and beat their male counterparts in a range of sports. I am often beaten by women tennis players, and no matter how hard I train, they will probably continue to beat me. Likewise, at the gym when instructors in HIIT classes or circuit classes suggest that women don't lift as heavy as the men, or go for less reps, then again there is an assumption that women cannot do the same as men even though this is not the case.

Lessons from the field

In this section I offer some lessons I have learnt from working in the space of LGBTI+ inclusion in Australia as practitioner and researcher:

1. *Administrators in Sport are crucial:* I have worked with numerous sport administrators across a wide range of sports organisations including National and State Sporting Organisations (NSOs/SSOs). Administrators hold the key to unlocking inclusion efforts, and are the gatekeepers into a sports organisation. These could be diversity and inclusion officers, the CEO's, or an LGBTI+ ally who works in marketing. Administrators have the ability and power to introduce and design new polices, allocate funding to an inclusive participation program, or help fund education to a range of clubs who want to be more LGBTI+ inclusive.

2. *The Business Case for LGBTI+ Diversity:* It took us about a year at Proud 2 Play to work out that promoting LGBTI+ inclusion from the social justice perspective and human rights approach did not hit the mark in trying to engage sports organisations. After a year or so of meetings,

pitches, hundreds of coffees, we radically changed how we approached sports organisations. We had to sell LGBTI+ inclusion as a product from the business case; sports administrators' key aim is to grow their sport, but also to make revenue. Engaging a market in which they have never engaged with before was scary, but an interesting prospect for many sports. We began to see a lot more traction when LGBTI+ inclusion was seen as good for their business, whilst ALSO doing good for wider society. The work of American scholar George Cunningham is useful for outlining how LGBTI+ diversity engagement in sport leads to higher organisational productivity.

3. *It's Good to Talk:* Sports do not respond well to either being called out for discriminatory practices or when they get things wrong; whether it be responding to an incident around homophobia, or a discriminatory policy around trans players. We need to avoid shouting down organisations and not offering alternatives or help in addressing their faults. People working in sport generally have little knowledge around LGBTI+ issues, and they often want to talk and learn about the area. But often they become scared to speak out or ask questions in case they are shot down or get things wrong. Overall in my experience, sports do not know how to do LGBTI+ inclusion. Therefore, we need to show them how to enact LGBTI+ inclusion within their organisations on a daily basis. Pride rounds are good and very much needed, but often they can become a substitute for action, and organisations can simply reduce LGBTI+ inclusion to a one-day event in the calendar. Embedding LGBTI+ inclusion across the institution will result in true social change.

4. *Institutional Support:* Having an ally or champion in an organisation is crucial, but to bring about real culture change, it requires a whole-of-organisation approach and institutional support. This is important so diversity and inclusion does not become the job of one person, but every person in the organisation. Having the support of the CEO and senior leadership is very important; if they are not on board, it becomes very difficult to engage in the space, including getting things signed off, allocating resources to an initiative or simply organising drinks and snacks at a LGBTI+ event.

5. *LGBTI+ visibility:* We need LGBTI+ people in decision making roles and to be present and visible within administrations across the sport sector. There are few out administrators within sport. Given sport has not always been as welcoming or a safe space for LGBTI+ people, it

is not surprising. We need to encourage LGBTI+ people to take jobs in sport, to volunteer in local community clubs, to coach their children's football or basketball team, to score or officiate a cricket match in their local community, to apply for CEO positions within professional sporting clubs, and to take up positions on boards. The more visibility and people we have taking up positions across the whole sport sector, the more we will see inclusive decision-making.

6. *Change IS happening:* Whilst often we might feel like we are going backwards, especially around trans inclusion, change is happening. We have lots of outputs and evidence of change at Proud 2 Play, through tangible programs, practices, the creation of new polices, pride rounds, or funding being directed towards LGBTI+ causes. In a recent study I led around LGBTI+ supporter groups in sport, with a focus on AFL, one participant highlighted that five years ago, we would never have been having these conversations… never mind pride rounds, supporter groups, or being invited to social functions as recognised members of LGBTI+ groups. Social change is messy and can take a long time (the marriage equality bill and progress there took over a decade). The fact discussions are taking place, and sports are engaging in the space, is a positive step forward. Whether sports are doing enough is a different question.

Conclusion

Sport is an important institution within Australia, and can help advance and achieve equality and equity within society. The fight for gender equality is currently at the forefront of that. A request I have for LGBTI+ inclusion efforts is to move the narrative away from a deficit discourse to an asset-based one, where LGBTI+ people are celebrated for achievements and contributions to sport. LGBTI+ people have positive experiences playing sport all across Australia; we need to hear more of those stories. We need to acknowledge that there are challenges and transphobia in particular is still extremely prevalent, but that sport can and does serve as a platform to address heath inequalities and offer social connections to those who might need them the most. My call to action is for anyone involved in sport across any level, to help ensure it is inclusive and welcoming, especially for LGBTI+ people. To get involved in the movement, head to Proud 2 Play's website: www.proud2play.org.au.

References

Centers for Disease Control and Prevention (2016) *Trends in prevalence of physical activity and sedentary behaviors national YRBS: 1991–2013.*

Centers for Disease Control and Prevention (2018) Youth Risk Behavior Surveillance—United States, 2017. *Morbidity and mortality weekly report. Surveillance summaries (Washington, D.C.: 2002), 67*(8), 1–114.

Doull, M., Watson, R.J., Smith, A., Homma, Y., Saewyc, E. (2018). Are we levelling the playing field? trends and disparities in sports participation among sexual minority youth in Canada. *Journal of Sport and Health Science, 7*(2), 218-226

Denison, E., & Kitchner, K. (2015) Out on the Fields. The First International Study on Homophobia in Sport, Sydney, Australia.

Hillier, L. (2005). Safe spaces: The upside of the image problem for same sex attracted young women playing Australian rules football. *Football Studies, 8*(2), 51-64.

Hillier, L., Jones, T. Monagle, M., Overton, N., Gahan, L., Blackman, J., & Mitchell, A. (2010) Writing themselves in 3: The third national study on the sexual health and wellbeing of same sex attracted and gender questioning young people. Melbourne: Australian Research Centre in Sex, Health and Society, La Trobe University.

Smith, E., Jones, T., Ward, R., Dixon, J., Mitchell, A., & Hillier, L. (2014). From Blues to Rainbows: The Mental health and wellbeing of gender diverse and transgender young people in Australia. Melbourne: The Australian Research Centre in Sex, Health, and Society.

Symons, C., Sbaraglia, M., Hillier, L., & Mitchell, A. (2010) *Come Out To Play. The sports experience of Lesbian, Gay, Bisexual and Transgender (LGBT) people in Victoria,* Institute of Sport, Exercise and Active Living, Victoria University, Melbourne, Australia.

Symons, C, O'Sullivan, G, Borkoles, E, Anderson, M and Polman, R, (2014) *Equal Play: The Impact of Homophobic Bullying during Sport and Physical Education Participation on Same-Sex-Attracted and Gender- Diverse Young Australians' Depression and Anxiety Levels.* Beyondblue, Melbourne.

Dr Ryan Storr of Western Sydney University is co-founder and director of Proud 2 Play, a LGBTI+ youth sport charity, which aims to increase participation in sport for LGBTI+ youth, their friends and families. This work has involved consultancy and partnerships with State and National Sporting Organisations and working with sports to engage them with LGBTI+ diversity. Proud 2 Play was a winner in the Vic Health Sport Innovation Challenge, in partnership with Cricket Victoria, and received a grant of $100,000 to run the 'Proud Cricket Program', an education and social cricket program for the Victoria LGBTI+ community.

FRANK BONNICI

Frank Bonnici is a Melbourne-based artist and life model. His artistic interest is in denaturalising the body to show how it is socially produced and understood. Line work is fundamental to both his aesthetic approach and as a metaphor of dis/connection. Many of his works focus on the human figure and are made at Last Peek Studio in Thornbury.

OPPOSITE PAGE: UNNAMED. FRANK BONNICI

ABOVE & OPPOSITE—UNNAMED IMAGES. FRANK BONNICI

PRIDE MARCHES ARE CONTESTED SPACE
Let's globalise the Auckland ban on uniformed police!

LISA FARRELL

I was 11 years old and sitting in a stuffy building full of worshippers praising God and telling me that I should love no one more than Him. It was Sunday February 4, 1996. On the other side of the city, where the breezes blow in from the bay, something was beginning — a parade. It was the first of its kind in Victoria. With a glint of oiled skin in sunlight, the twirl of a boa, and the rev of a motorbike, Melbourne's first Pride March kicked off. It was full of potential, bringing together over 85 different LGBT groups from around Victoria. Among those who assembled in the park near Albert Park Lake, a group of fiery socialist feminists from Radical Women led a contingent, shouting 'Fund hospitals, not race tracks!' This brought applause from participants and spectators who loved the message linked to community opposition to the precinct being fenced off annually by profiteers during the Grand Prix. Melbourne's first Pride March was radical and anti-corporate to its roots.

The Melbourne Pride march will kick off again this year on 3 February with the rev of a motorbike. But the iconic Dykes on Bikes will be closely followed by blue uniforms, batons, and semi-automatics. The Victoria Police will be followed by contingents from banks and corporations as well as politicians who were nowhere to be seen before they discovered there were votes to be had by backing the LGBTIQA+ community.

Early pride marches were crucial to making the LGBTIQA+ community visible and putting their issues at the forefront of discussion. They raised demands and generated much-needed organising for reforms to laws and policies. They created an environment where people could feel safe to come out, a crucial component of instigating widespread change in community attitudes. Each year organisations like Radical Women boldly inject intersectional, socialist feminist politics into Pride marches in an effort to keep the revolutionary activist spirit alive in Pride. But it is becoming more difficult with the heightened emphasis placed on big business, politicians and cops.

Pride marches are important for our community: before LGBTIQA+ voices can be heard, the diverse community must be visible. The concept of Pride is international: our need to be accepted on our own terms spans continents. Marching for LGBTIQA+ liberation happens in every corner of the world. The first Pride march in Jerusalem in 2002 was themed *Love without Borders*. In a show of defiance, Jews and a few Arabs, who managed to get through the checkpoints, marched together to demand LGBT rights, peace and justice for Palestinians. Later marches featured united contingents of Palestinian and anti-Zionist Jews.

Marches have taken place across the continent of Africa in countries as diverse as Mauritius, South Africa, Swaziland and Uganda. Addressing local issues, each protested horrific treatment of LGBTIQA+ people, advocated rights and provided visibility. Across Asia, Pride marches are now a feature in many countries including Japan, India, the Philippines, Taiwan, Thailand and Vietnam. In 2017, Timor-Leste had their very first Pride march with 500 people marching in Dili. Marches have occurred all over Europe too: the most recent having started in both Greenland and Lithuania in 2010. While these Pride marches are filled with people from many different cultures, backgrounds and experiences, they all have one thing in common: they began as a political protest for better treatment of LGBTIQA+ people and to increase our visibility. We are everywhere!

What's in a name? The taming and corporatising of Pride

These grassroots groundswells of political activity pave the way for more rights and freedoms, but what happens when they lose their political focus and start to become a drawcard for companies seeking to profit from the pink dollar? Instead of being about inclusivity, visibility and organising, they become easily digestible tourist attractions to market to gawking crowds. Politicians start using Pride marches to advertise their party. Corporations put their rainbow flags everywhere and scream, 'Look at us, look how good we are, we're throwing a rainbow coloured bone your way. Support us!' We can see this seismic shift as the goal of Pride marches becomes **contested** space within the LGBTIQA+ communities. The well-to-do in the community start to become comfortable

reaping the benefits of growing visibility and acceptance. While for
the most oppressed members of the community, the aim is
liberation: homophobia and transphobia remain a layer of
oppression as they navigate life in a grossly unequal world.

Pride marches in Tel Aviv and Jerusalem, which have united
LGBTIQA+ Palestinians and anti-Zionist Jews, have come under
sustained criticism by LGBTIQA+ activists as 'pinkwashing.' This is
where Israel is portrayed as a haven for LGBT people within a
hostile Middle East, while the demands of LGBT Palestinians are
disappeared and the oppression and discrimination against
Palestinians ignored. The Pride march in London has also been
condemned for embracing a form of rainbow and pinkwashing.
Corporations like British Airways and United States Airlines
participate in London Pride. These are the airlines of choice used by
governments to deport LGBTIQA+ refugees to countries where
their lives are in danger. These are just two examples of how some
in the LGBTIQA+ community are left out when Pride marches are
monetised and when they lose sight of their radical roots. This trend
is global.

Resistance is fabulous!

There is one country that is currently setting an example of how
Pride marches can reclaim themselves from corporations and
groups that oppress and marginalise LGBTIQA+ people — New
Zealand. Last November, the Auckland Pride board voted to ban
police from marching in uniform in 2019. Members of the police
force could attend as citizens, but not in uniform. The police in all
countries are used to protect the assets of the rich, while limiting the
freedoms of the marginalised. Police forces particularly target
LGBTIQA+ communities and make them feel unsafe. From the
Stonewall Riots in New York, the Tasty nightclub raid in
Melbourne, to the consistent maltreatment of Maori LGBTIQA+
people, police forces have never worked for or supported
LGBTIQA+ communities.

Auckland Pride recognised that the police force visibility
participating in the march puts some in their community at risk.
Their official statement said, 'as an institution [NZ Police] do not
currently meet the degree of safety and awareness of
intersectionality required by our rainbow communities.' With this
simple and factual statement, all hell broke loose with conservatives
fomenting a backlash by corporations, banks, and the New Zealand

police force. In response to the NZ police being banned from marching in uniform, major corporations and banks withdrew their sponsorship in retaliation. This response highlights that corporate sponsorship always comes with strings. Organisations that are genuinely inclusive and supportive of the LGBTIQA+ community would understand the threat of police to participant safety. Supporters wouldn't withdraw backing just because they don't like a decision made by organisers — in this case, a careful and reasoned one. Organisations and corporations that remove their support are fair-weather friends who disappear as soon as they perceive there is no advantage for them to remain.

The good news is that there is massive support for the Auckland Pride board's decisions. Auckland Pride considered withdrawing the option of corporate sponsorship and turned to the community for support. By the end of November, more than $13,000 was raised through crowdfunding. In December, more than 1,200 people turned up to an Auckland Pride meeting where a motion of no confidence in the board was on the agenda. This was roundly defeated with the community backing the Pride Board's decision to ban uniformed police. The Auckland Pride march will take place on 16 February.

Rebuilding the revolution

With the new year just beginning, we have the opportunity in Australia to reclaim our roots for the Pride marches. We can see the example set by the Auckland Pride board as a stepping stone to creating a more inclusive, radical, brilliant Pride that embraces all members of the LGBTIQA+ community, and not simply those members who have the most appeal to conservative Australia and the most to spend with big business sponsors. We won't know the full ramifications of the decision made by the Auckland Pride board until their march occurs, but we do know that the LGBTIQA+ people participating will feel safe, heard and visible. With the twirl of a boa, the rev of a motorcycle and the wide-eyed amazement of an 11-year-old sitting on a patch of grass in the sunlight, rather than in a stuffy church, let's show the world what it really means to have ***Pride!***

Lisa Farrell coordinates Radical Women's work in the LGBTIQA+ community. Contact her at radicalwomen@optusnet.com.au
This piece was first published in the **Freedom Socialist Organiser** # 30, January 2019. You can subscribe to the Organiser at https://socialism.com/subscribe-to-the-fso/

WHAT LGBT PARENTS WANT IN SCHOOLS
TRENT MANN, TIFFANY JONES

Changes in how LGBT parents are viewed

LGBT parents are becoming increasingly common in Australian schooling communities (ABS, 2013; Dempsey, 2013; Perlesz, et al. 2010). Research has not explored the ability for schooling communities and institutions to reflect the now greater levels of acceptance and the push for inclusive supports for LGBT parents (Leland, 2017; Mercier & Harold, 2003). This research is particularly pertinent as attitudes, beliefs and stereotypes of Australians seem to have changed in recent years (ABS, 2017). This article reports on a survey of LGBT parents designed to understand their views on supports.

Literature on LGBT parents influencing schools

The literature on LGBT parents stems mainly from U.S. and U.K. samples emerging from the 1960s, with growing literature from Australia (Goldberg, 2011; Kosciw & Diaz, 2008; Lindsay, et al. 2006). The research into LGBT parents has developed from anecdotal aetiological studies to exploring LGBT parent experiences within specific contexts. There are four main types of dominant conceptual framings for studies on LGBT parents (see Table 1). Over time, the emphasis has variably included:

- Anti-LGBT Studies—which take an outright negative view of the group's identities;
- LGBT Parent and Child Development Studies—which show some suspicion towards the group's influence on kids;
- LGBT Parented Family Diversity and Family Functioning Studies—which consider the group's experiences of stigmatisation; and
- LGBT Parents in School Contexts Studies—which consider discrimination.

All of these conceptualisations focus on negative framings of LGBT parent identities or experiences, showing a suspicion of the possibilities for the group itself or their engagement with their children's worlds. Power et al.'s (2012) study differed in how it showed the internal resilience of the group across their experiences; however, following Gahan's (2017) exploration of external provisions broadly, we saw a need to study assistance for the group in school services specifically.

New tasks for LGBT parents studies

Farr, Tasker & Goldberg (2017) state current studies on LGBT parented families have focussed on addressing public debates of sexual minority parent family structures without theoretical frameworks informing research. Whilst there are clearly many ideas on what might support LGBT parents in schools emerging—policies, staff training and so forth; the impacts of such supports for LGBT parents in practice are not yet directly 'research-based' or 'research-proven'. The perspectives of LGBT parents on the benefits of inclusive school strategies have been overlooked in previous research (Cloughessy & Waniganayake, 2013). Studies now must aim to *focus on the impacts of supportive factors and the ideals for supports that LGBT parents themselves can lend insight on,* contrasting to existing literature adopting a largely *deficit approach* to LGBT parents in school contexts, and overlooking supportive constructs that may offset the stressors experienced by LGBT parents. There is also a diversity to LGBT parents—often treated as a homogenous group (Perlesz et al., 2010)—which must not be overlooked.

Further, Farr, Tasker and Goldberg (2017) point out that theoretical frameworks were inadequately applied or absent from most LGBT parenting research. Robinson (2002) argues ecological theory offers a more detailed conceptualisation of family engagement within institutions; directly applicable to considering LGBT parents' needs in schools. Bronfenbrenner's ecological theory (1974) could particularly be developed to generate new research in the field (Farr, Goldberg & Tasker, 2017). Bronfenbrenner states that an individual is nested within five broad ecological systems (See Figure 1). At the centre is the **Individual** (e.g. an LGBT parent), including all their characteristics. The study was mainly concerned with the **Microsystem** level of external influence surrounding LGBT parents which included environmental variables that directly interact with the individuals and their families.

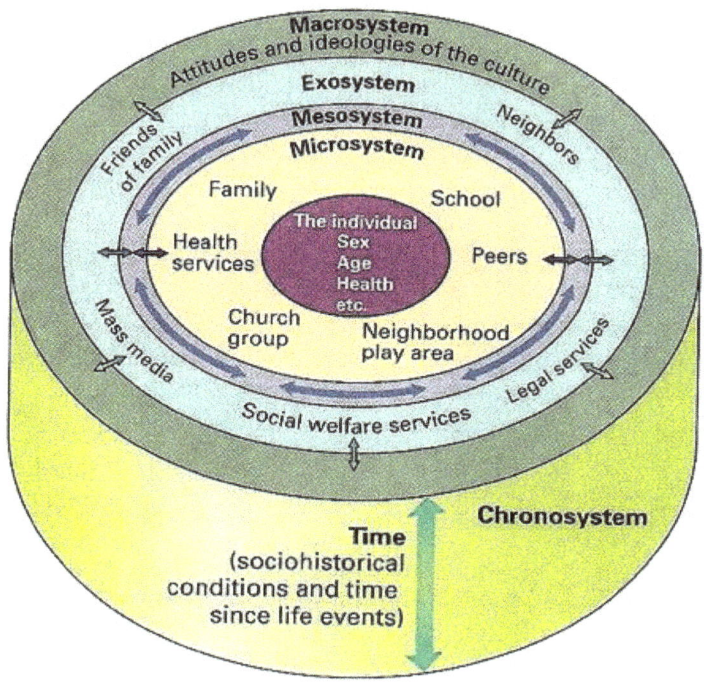

Figure 1: Bronfenbrenner's Ecological Theory of Development (1974, p.47).

Survey methodology

A mix of qualitative and quantitative data have the potential to provide stronger results by drawing on the strengths of each (Creswell & Garrett, 2008; Creswell & Plano Clark, 2011; Johnson, Onwuegbuzie, & Turner 2007). For this study, since psychological and social phenomena are inherently complex, and because multiple sexuality and gender groups were being included, both qualitative and quantitative were necessary to best draw out differing experiences and perspectives (Creswell & Garrett, 2008; Creswell & Plano Clark, 2011). An online survey was developed to explore the demographic diversity of Australian LGBT parents, their child's school characteristics and their perceptions of the benefits of various supports in Australian schools. Care was taken to ensure the survey did not rely on schools as distributors, as discussion of sexuality and gender themes in education settings can embarrass LGBT people, or expose them to stigma and discrimination (UNESCO, 2019, p.16). A *qualitatively driven* mixed method design was selected for the survey, to employ the strengths of quantitative and qualitative research (Johnson & Christensen, 2014). This allowed open questioning to capture the complexities of sex and gender identity likely to be seen across a mixed LGBT group.

Participants were recruited from the general Australian LGBT parent community with children in Australian schools via convenience and snowballing non-random sampling techniques for 10 days in 2019. In total, 150 complete and incomplete surveys were submitted to Qualtrics. However after the removal of non-responses and those outside the target group, the participants included 73 LGBT parents with children currently enrolled in Australian schools. Analysis of responses to open-eneded questions was aided by Leximancer, which identified the dominant themes and most typical quote excerpts for each theme. This is useful for ensuring the research did not focus only on outlier, emotive examples, and considered what was most common.

LGBT parent demographics

Participants were aged 25-64yrs of age, and almost half of the sample were 35-44yrs (Table 1). They were mostly located in eastern states; primarily Queensland followed by New South Wales, Victoria, South Australia, Western Australia and the Northern Territory. The gender of parents in the sample was predominantly female followed by male, other and transgender. Of those who responded 'other', four respondents identified as non-binary, one as trans-male, one as trans-female and one as female-bodied. The sample was predominantly affluent and highly educated. Nearly 70% of the sample earned annual incomes over $90,000 and over 60% held university (undergraduate and postgraduate) qualifications. Close to 70% of the participants were in married or committed relationships followed by divorced, another option and single. Of those participants selecting 'another option', five were dating, three were single and one was in a polyamorous relationship. Table 2 also shows over half of participants identified as Atheist, followed by Christianity, another option, Agnostic/undecided, Judaism and Islam. Of the four indicating another option, six identified as pagan, two as none, one as yoga and one as ex-Christian. Most participants indicated having two or more children. The age of participants youngest child ranged from 0-18yrs; most children were aged under 14yrs.

Table 1

AGE		INCOME	
25-34yrs	16.4%	Less than $30,000	8.2%
35-44yrs	48.0%	$30,000-$59,999	8.2%
45-54yrs	31.5%	$60,000-$89,999	13.7%
55-64yrs	4.1%	Over $90,000	67.1%
		Prefer not to say	2.7%

SEXUAL ORIENTATION		EDUCATION	
Lesbian	61.6%	Up to 4 yrs high school	2.4%
Another option	13.7%	Completed high school	9.6%
Gay	12.3%	Diploma or certificate	21.9%
Bisexual	12.3%	Undergraduate degree	24.7%
		Postgraduate degree	41.1%

RELATIONSHIP STATUS		RELIGION	
Single, never married	4.1%	Christianity	14.5%
Married, or defacto	68.5%	Judaism	1.5%
Divorced, separated	15.1%	Islam	1.5%
Another option	12.3%	Atheist/None	56.5%
		Agnostic/Undecided	11.6%
		Another option	14.5%

STATE		AGE OF YOUNGEST CHILD	
New South Wales	23.3%	0-4yrs	27.4%
Northern Territory	1.4%	5-9yrs	42.5%
Queensland	37.0%	10-14yrs	23.3%
South Australia	9.6%	15-18yrs	6.8%
Victoria	23.3%		
Western Australia	5.5%		

NUMBER OF CHILDREN	
1	31.5%
2	39.7%
3 or more	28.8%

Microsystems—school type, location & supports

The physical characteristics of LGBT parent school microsystems are displayed in Table 2. The majority of children in the sample were enrolled in Public schools, followed by Catholic, Independent and Other. Of those respondents who indicated other, one was in a special needs school and one was in an Anglican private school. Over 60% of the sample had children enrolled in primary school, followed by Kindergarten/Prep, and high-school. The majority of the sample had children enrolled in schools in outer metropolitan areas, followed by regional, inner metropolitan and rural locations.

Table 2

CATEGORY	%
Child's school type	
Public	69.9%
Independent	13.7%
Catholic	13.7%
Other	2.7%
Child's Grade	
Kindergarten/Preparatory	17.8%
1-3	30.1%
4-6	36.9%
7-10	8.2%
11-12	6.9%
Location of School	
Inner Metropolitan	28.8%
Outer Metropolitan	35.6%
Regional	31.5%
Rural/Remote	4.1%

The microsystem environmental characteristics of participants were explored by asking about LGBT parents awareness of their child's school providing supportive strategies identified in school guide research. As can be seen in Figure 2, inclusive school forms (27.8%) was the most common supportive strategy present in schools followed by items that reflect LGBT families in classrooms (19.3%), specific mention of LGBT families in school policy (14.8%), teacher training in LGBT topics/issues (12.3%), lessons on LGBT topics (8.9%) and mention of LGBT family structures in school brochures/documents (7.0%). The least likely school supports provided for by schools included mention of LGBT families in brochures or documents (73.7%), followed by LGBT inclusive curriculum (62.0%), items that reflect LGBT families (53.5%), LGBT inclusive school forms (50.4%), LGBT families in school policy (50.4%) and teacher training in LGBT topics or issues (26.3%).

There was a significant amount of uncertainty in the sample regarding the provision of many supports: particularly teacher training in LGBT topics/ issues (61.4%) and explicit mention of LGBT families in school policy (34.8%), followed by LGBT lessons (29.2%),

LGBT reflective items in classrooms (27.19%), LGBT inclusive forms
and documents (21.74%) and mention of LGBT families in brochures
or websites (19.3%).

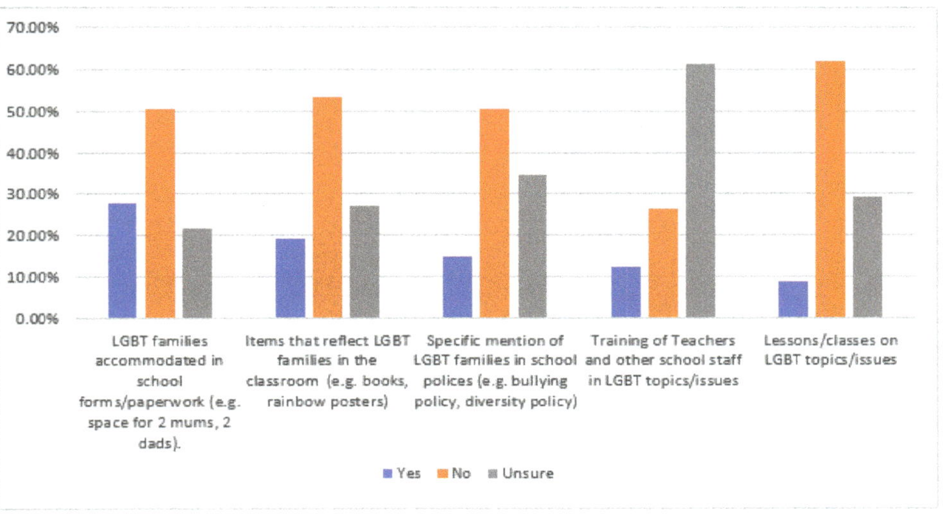

Figure 2: Support strategies reported by Australian LGBT parents in schools

LGBT parents on the usefulness of supports

Table 3 shows that over 80% of LGBT parents deemed all suggested
supportive strategies as important and beneficial in forming positive
school environments; teacher training and LGBT inclusive forms
were unanimously affirmed. In the comments, LGBT parents showed
concern that teacher training needed to discuss the range of family
constellations rather than present a homonormative ideal whether
they mentioned single parents or indigenous kinship models. In the
most typical examples according to computer analysis, Kerry (46 yrs,
Victoria) said *'it should be embedded in being educated in broader not common
family structures, ie accepting of diverse family structures not just LGBT'*; Sophia
(38 yrs, Queensland) said, *'there is a risk that education like this becomes
tokenistic. LGBT families are as diverse as any other family. There is a risk that
assumptions are made'*. This concern for diverse family structures was
also shown in the comments on forms. Trinity (50 yrs, Victoria) said
*'I often have to modify forms in order to accurately describe the relationship between
my son and my partner'* and Ben (49 yrs, Queensland) commented that

some issues could easily be resolved since *'forms can easily be gender inclusive (simple language such as parent)'*.

Table 3

Perceived importance and benefit of supportive structures in school environments.

	LGBT parent perceptions of School supportive strategies			
	IMPORTANCE		BENEFIT	
Support strategies	*yes*	*no*	*beneficial*	*unproductive*
Teacher training	100.0%	*	100.0%	*
LGBT inclusive forms	100.0%	*	100.0%	*
Items that reflect LGBT families	95.9%	4.1%	95.9%	4.1%
LGBT families in website	86.3%	13.7%	90.4%	9.6%
LGBT inclusive school policies	83.6%	16.4%	90.4%	9.6%
LGBT inclusive curriculum	80.8%	19.2%	88.7%	11.3%

Positive experiences & future hopes

Most (51 of the 73) participants reported that they had positive one-off or person-specific positive experiences within schools (17 said no, 5 did not respond). The predominant theme was instances of staffs' sensitive treatment of the families during days most likely to cause distress or difficulty. For example, Zoey (46yrs, NSW) said *'At our intake interview our daughters' whole family was welcomed; this included lesbian mum, trans parent and her two dads … was just a non-issue'*. Mary (37yrs, Victoria) said, *'They are always accommodating around Mother's day and Father's Day'* (Mary, 37yrs, Victoria). Some parents talked about particular teachers who were very careful to be inclusive in their language use or consultative around complex issues—asking the parents directly how best to proceed regarding gendered events or family days. Only a few individuals had a positive experience of the 'plebiscite'—the least dominant theme. The positive experiences revolved around instances where schools took steps to address the potential negative impact of the plebiscite. For example, Fiona (37yrs, South Australia) stated *'during the plebiscite the principal several times checked in with us to see how we were travelling and if we were being too badly impacted, which was just lovely'*, and Violet (36yrs, Victoria) noted *'The school chaplain released a lovely article to parents during the plebiscite to support the local lgbti community which was nice'*. John (47yrs, Victoria) responded *'Lots of support during the marriage equality plebiscite. Lots of support and questions in discussing our son's 2 dad family'*.

However, the majority of LGBT parents (39 of 73) did not feel they were included overall in schools; most answered the question on whether they were generally included within the school simply with 'no'. Participants were asked 'Please list any suggestions you have for schools or teachers, in terms of making LGBT parented families feel more welcome in your child's school community'. Most participants (52) had suggestions; the most dominant being improved inclusive school treatment—for their 'kids' (34 Hits), 'families' (30 Hits) or for 'inclusive' (22 Hits) goals broadly. Arguments within this theme include examples of where the lack of inclusion of different family types in activities/interpersonal practices within the microsystem can cause inadvertent exclusion of children due to family formations. Thematically typical quotes included examples of moments where inclusion was disrupted:

> One day, a teacher asked 'Hands up if you do chores for your Mum and Dada'. Our youngest kept her hand down—not because she doesn't do chores but because she thought they were asking if she had a Mum and Dad. A section in the curriculum on ancestry caused some problems because the teacher just hadn't thought through what that looked like for kids living with one or more non-genetic parents. They were receptive but a little naïve (Hope, 35yrs, Queensland).

Rebecca (37yrs, Northern Territory) wanted:

> Just more understanding from outsiders who generalize and have misconceptions of family. One incident with a teacher which upset our child would have been avoided if they asked our child for an explanation (Rebecca, 37yrs, Northern Territory).

Several parents discussed concerns their child could be bullied, and pushed for a 'zero tolerance' approach where any harm to their kids was concerned.

Discussion & conclusion

Whilst previous research mostly represented parents in Victoria, South Australia and New South Wales (Lindsay et al. 2006; Cloughessy et al. 2018; Cloughessy et al. 2019) this study represents a stronger sample from Queensland. The predominance of child enrolment in public schools is similar to recent Australian census data (ABS, 2018) reporting 65.7% of students are enrolled in public schools—this reflected that parents were not necessarily avoiding independent schools despite the possibility for their exemption from serving LGBT parents where religious grounds are sought.

This research adds to previous studies showing LGBT parents earn above-average incomes and have higher qualifications in education compared to dual-gendered parents (ABS, 2016; Crouch, et al. 2014). This may be reflective of the costly nature of conceiving children in same-sex attracted relationships such as IVF, clinic-based insemination and surrogacy agreements (Crouch et al. 2014). Despite efforts at including diverse parents, the group was dominated by wealthier older lesbians, as noted elsewhere (e.g. Power et al. 2010). However, the participants' comments showed a strong resistance to 'norms' about LGBT parents being pushed through schools or research, and a sensitivity to the idea that families come in many forms including single parent, multi-parent, adoptive, indigenous kinship and other types of guardian arrangements. This appreciation of broader family diversities is a feature of LGBT parents.

The study echoed a US finding by Kosciw & Diaz (2008) that less than a third of schools provided lessons inclusive of LGBT topics and only 10% of parents were aware of teacher training in LGBT topics. It shows that teacher training and form inclusion were especially beneficial to LGBT parents despite their low occurrence and attacks on bodies like the Safe Schools Coalition enabling such support previously. Their suggestions for improving schools were focused on supports which would directly better their children's experiences. Whilst many LGBT parents have had some specific positive experiences, their own and their children's sense of a lack of overall inclusion came through regardless of the studies' affirming emphasis. This shows that the lack of broad inclusion for LGBT parents and families in schools is *not a product of research methods or emphases*. It is a material reality that needs to be addressed not only by those particular teachers and principals who make an effort sometimes, but across education systems. Bronfenbrenner's 'macrosystems' including cultural attitudes and 'exosystems' including the media will have a role to play in encouraging change at this broader level; especially the push for system-level roll out of teacher training, updated form templates and the clear communication of other wide-reaching institutional efforts in all education sectors to stem current confusion on where schools stand.

References

Australian Bureau of Statistics. (2018, 06 1). *1800.0 Australian Marriage Law Postal Survey, 2017*. Retrieved from: www.abs.gov.au

Australian Bureau of Statistics. (2018, 06 1). *410.2.0 Austrealian Social Trends, July 2013*. Retrieved from Australian Bureau of Statistics: www.ABS.gov.au

Bronfrenbrenner, U. (1974). Developmental research, public policy and the ecology of childhood. *Child Development*, 1-5.

Cloughessy, K., & Waniganayake, M. (2013). Early childhood educators working with children who have lesbian, gay, bisexual and transgender parents: What does the literature tell us? *Early Child Development and Care*, 1-10.

Creswell, J. W., & Garrett, A. L. (2008). The' movement' of mixed methods research and the role of educators. *South African Journal of Education*, 28(3), 321– 333. Retrieved from http://www.scielo.org.za

Creswell, J. W., & Plano Clark, V. L. (2011). Choosing a mixed methods design. In J. W. Creswell & V. L. Plano Clark, *Designing and conducting mixed methods research* (2nd ed.) (pp. 53-106). Los Angeles, CA: SAGE Publications.

Dempsey, D. (2013). Same-sex parented families in Australia. *Australian Institute of Family Studies: Child Family Community Australia (18)*, 1-26.

Farr, R., Tasker, F., & Goldberg, A. (2017). Theory in highly cited studies of sexual minority parent families: Variations and implications. *Journal of Homosexuality*, 1143-1179.

Gahan, L. (2017). Seperated same-sex parents' experiences and views of services and service providers. *Journal of Family Strengths*, 1-34.

Goldberg, A. E., & Smith, J. Z. (2011). Stigma, social context, and mental health: Lesbian and gay couples across the transition to adoptive parenthood. *Journal of Counselling Psychology*, 139-150.

Goldberg, A. E., & Smith, J. Z. (2014). Preschool selection considerations and experiences of school mistreatment among lesbian, gay, and heterosexual adoptive parents. *Early Childhood Research Quarterly*, 64-75.

Johnson, B., & Christensen, L. (2014). *Educational Research: Quantitative, Qualitative, and Mixed Approaches*. London; United Kingdom: SAGE Publications.

Johnson, R. B., Onwuegbuzie, A. J., & Turner, L. A. (2007). Toward a definition of mixed methods research. *Journal of Mixed Methods Research*, 1(2), 112–133.

Kosciw, J. G., & Diaz, E. M. (2008). *Involved, Invisible, Ignored: The Experiences of Lesbian, Gay, Bisexual and Transgender Parents and Their Children in Our Nation's L-12 Schools*. New York: GLSEN.

Leland, A. (2017). Navigating gay fatherhood: The experiences of four sets of gay fathers with their children's education. *Gender and Education*, 632-647.

Lindsay, J., Perlesz, A., Brown, R., McNair, R., de Vaus, D., & Pitts, M. (2006). Stigma or Respect: Lesbian-parented Families Negotiating School Settings. *Sociology*, 1059-1077.

Mercier, L., & Harold, R. (2003). At the interface: Lesbian-Parent families and their children's schools. *Children & Schools*, 35-47.

Perlesz, A., Power, J. B., McNair, R., Schofield, M., Pitts, M., Barrett, A., & Bickerdlike, A. (2010). Organising work and home in same-sex parented families: FIndings from the work love play study. *The Australian and New Zealand Journal of Family Therapy*, 374-391.

Power, J., Perlesz, A., Brown, R. S., Pitts, M., McNair, R., & Bickerdike, A. (2010a). Diversity, tradition and family: Australian same-sex attracted parents and their families. *Gay & Lesbian Issues and Psychology Review*, 66-81.

Power, J., Perlesz, A., McNair, R., Schofield, M., Pitts, M., Brown, R., & Bickeerdike, A. (2012). Gay and bisexual dads and diversity: Fathers in the work, love, play study. *Journal of Family Studies*, 143-154.

Robinson, K. (2002). Making the invisible visible: Gay and lesbian issues in early childhood. *Contemporary Issues in Early Childhood*, 415-434.

UNESCO (2019). *Bringing it Out in the Open: Monitoring school violence based on sexual orientation, gender identity or gender expression in national and international surveys*. Paris: UNESCO.

Trent Mann is a higher degree research student at Macquarie University who completed his Masters-level survey of lesbian, gay, bisexual and transgender parents in 2019. He has engaged in study in the Graduate Diploma in Education Studies at QUT, Bachelor of Psychological Sciences (Hons) at Federation University, Graduate Diploma in Psychology University of Melbourne and Bachelor of Business (Hons) La Trobe. Past theses have included 'The Influence of Academic Achievement and Classroom Environments on Solitary Behaviour in Anxious Solitary Children' and 'The Moderating Role of Organisational Communication and Mediating Role of Job Interdependence on Job Satisfaction in a Small to Medium Australian Manufacturing Firm'.

EVERYONE IS SOUTH OF CHINA
JASON LI

My phone lights up with tiny grey speech bubbles as the Hong Kong and Chinese student fists hit the Hong Kong and Chinese student faces at the University of Queensland, across the early weeks of August 2019. The texts are from frightened Aussie students who had been jostled as they walked past hundreds of warring Asians in the campus courtyards. They admit to me, their bisexual male business student friend from Hong Kong, that they don't understand these battles or the nationalistic chanting from the Chinese kids of 'China is great'. They ask me outright what is going on. Some of the organisers of the rally were objecting to the university's links to the Chinese government; attempting to hold sit-ins in front of the Beijing-funded Confucius Institute (Hunter, 2019). In response to my reply, my friends type: 'But Jase, aren't the Hong Kongers and the Taiwanese chanting their national songs back at those kids, actually Chinese too?'

I restrain myself from texting back that if Hong Kong and Taiwan *being located South of China* makes those countries Chinese, then Australia is China too. We all sit within the endlessly expanding imagined boundaries of this aggressor's 'South China Sea'. China is intent on expanding ever Southward, having partnered with Russia to the North ... I hover my thumbs above my phone's keypad envisioning myself sending what I am typing: 'Guys, *YOU'RE* South of China'. I don't press send. These naive Aussie kids just wouldn't understand the gallows humour.

When you live relatively comfortable lives like my straight white Aussie pals, you don't think to keep an eye out over your shoulder for the barrel of a gun, and only noticing one when you've accidentally wandered into the direct red line of its laser target designator. These straight kids share my lecture halls, but without knowing it they also share my reality of the very real threat an aggressive China poses to the security of their democratic world. They don't pore over news articles and film clips searching for the faces of people they grew up with getting squashed by the batons of Chinese Communist Party aggression. They don't worry about whether their relationship rights will be echoed within the laws of their country. They watch Australian opinion shows like *Q&A* where presenters like Tony Jones can ask

Trumpian questions like if there was violence on 'both sides' of events where the Chinese Communist Party organises attacks on both Hong Kong and Australian student protesters on Australian soil—limiting Australian students' freedom of speech (Wolfe, 2019). They don't fret that if their nation was invaded from the North their existing freedoms could be closed down with a push of a button like the glorious yellow fabric of yesterday's umbrella, restrained with its own cord and folded away forever.

It's different for my Aussie gay friends. Being more battle-hardened in the realm of rights, they are usually at least broadly aware that there have been pro-democracy protests in Hong Kong. Some even know of the yellow umbrella grass-roots rights movement of recent years pushing against authoritarian Chinese rule in favour of Hong Kong sovereignty (Ma & Cheung, 2019), and they have been texting me umbrella emojis. They usually understand that the majority of Hong Kong citizens seek to avoid becoming subsumed into China under the rule of the Chinese Communist Party, after being released from British colonisation and promised the integrity of our own separate system of rule. Gay Aussies especially seem to comprehend that as someone whose same sex relationships are not currently treated the same in my home country's laws, I am deeply attached to the potentials of my nation remaining a democracy. My life will be shaped by the outcomes of the last 11 weeks of demonstrations against a proposed extradition bill (Kuo, 2019). My gay Aussie friends seem to appreciate that in the long run, the loss of my rights affects the certainty of their own.

If Hong Kong agrees to extradite any of our citizens who are targeted as 'wanted' (read: human rights activists) to China, no Hong Kong citizen will be free. Especially not LGBTIQ people. We will no longer be able to congregate in public pride parades; gathering in public is seen as a threat to Beijing's rule. We will no longer be able to continue making gains in our fight for local relationship rights in lawsuits; like Angus Leung and Scott Adams who, having married in New Zealand in 2014, recently succeeded in pushing for civil servant spousal benefits and joint taxation status in a Hong Kong Final Court of Appeals for themselves … and by extension, other same-sex married couples (Chandran, 2019). The LGBTIQ leaders currently looking to run the 2022 Gay Games Australians are looking to attend (Out in Hong Kong, 2019), could face cancellation as with earlier hoped-for Gay Games, re-education camps at best and, at worst, potential execution on some false pretext.

My gay Aussie friends ask me questions: whether I will be in danger if I go back home as a bisexual man? And whether they would be in danger visiting me there? They believe me when I say 'yes'. It is hard to argue that Hong Kong will remain a democracy for long if such a significant portion of its population—around two million of its approx. 7million citizens (Lee, Li, & Kwan, 2019)—can mobilise against a bill without results. And if another nation can simply take, and lock up, our activists. And if we can demand, but be beaten by armed foreign forces out of achieving, our own systems of law… as our local police stand by and do nothing to protect us.

We live in unprecedented times where the US and UK have weakened, and a new world order is pending. The precise hierarchy is however unclear. New democracies around the world are under threat at the time when their greatest achievements for LGBTIQ people are now visibly within their grasps. We are making decisions about what and who we will stand up for, when really what we stand for should be everything and who we stand for, everyone. Populations that accept losses to LGBTIQ rights and cultural diversity movements at the time provide the key linchpin signifying the acceptance of autocratic factions and external incursions. Populations that accept or don't notice external interference, will see it increased exponentially. Homophobia and transphobia are key forms of interference.

That's why I want LGBTIQ Australians to really sit up and take notice of the China-backed politicians who use homophobia and transphobia as a way to launch social media attacks on gay Hong Kong pro-democracy protest organisers. One example has been pro-establishment legislator Ann Chiang Lai-wan, who shared footage on Facebook of gay activist and Hong Kong protest leader Jimmy Sham (of the Civil Human Rights Front and rights group Rainbow Action). The clip showed Jimmy in drag. She posted the words: 'Important news, please spread around' (Asli, 2019). She accused him of hiding his sexual orientation and incited commenters—whether these were real people or perhaps funded Chinese online propagandists—to describe him as 'corrupting' and 'disgusting'. However, Jimmy Sham was actually out and open about his sexuality. Chiang's charges of Sham's concealment of his private life, which would not have been a crime, were actually bogus. This attack was then featured in the South China Morning Post (Asli, 2019). There was some back and forth between Chiang and Sham across July this year that showed Chiang's belief Sham could not complain about her attacks, given he was out... which to me really showed how old-world autocracies will always seek to squash diversity so central to the new worlds' democracies through unapologetic discrimination. Ultimately LGBTI rights activists appealed to the city's equality watchdog. Finally, Facebook took the post down on the basis that it 'does not allow content that attacks someone based on their sexual orientation'. LGBTIQ Australians should note that there have also been similarly homophobic interference attacks made by China on Australian labour politicians and democratic rule during the 2019 election; including the accusations on Webo that Bill Shorten pushes gay sex on kids (Cannane & Hui, 2019; Tomazin & Zhuang, 2019).

I text back to my Aussie friends that although the Hong Kong leadership are verbally promising to shelve the extradition law after mass protests, we Hong Kongers want it completely withdrawn and we want a democratic nation. China's courts are considered neither free nor fair; its politicians use homophobia and transphobia as one of many weapons for human rights violations. When the UK handed Hong Kong back to China in 1997, China agreed to govern Hong Kong under a 'one country, two systems' policy for at least half a century. Hong Kongers were not to be subjected to Chinese law and to retain our own levels of freedom of the press and free speech. China has so completely broken this pact that we must consider the deal as 'off'.

Now the obvious question that remains is: how far South of China would an LGBTIQ friendly democracy need to be to remain free from anti-rights and discriminatory interference? If there is no answer, we may need to start asking a lot more questions.

References

Asli, A. (2019). Hong Kong lawmaker Ann Chiang and Civil Human Rights Front convenor Jimmy Sham locked in heated Facebook row over his sexual orientation. *South China Morning Post*. Accessed 21.7.19. Retrieved from https://today.line.me/id/pc/article/Hong+Kong+lawmaker+Ann+Chiang+and+Civil+Human+Rights+Front+convenor+Jimmy+Sham+locked+in+heated+Facebook+row+over+his+sexual+orientation-QQx2Dp

Cannane, S., & Hui, E. (2019). Federal election 2019: Anti-Labor scare campaign targets Chinese-Australians. *ABC Investigations*. Accessed 3.5.19. Retrieved from https://www.abc.net.au/news/2019-05-03/federal-election-scare-campaign-targets-chinese-australians/11073514

Chandran, R. (2019). Hong Kong Court Favors Gay Couple In Landmark Victory For LGBTQ Rights. *Huffington Post*. Accessed 6.7.19. Retrieved from https://www.huffpost.com/entry/hong-kong-lgbtq-victory_n_5cfac2e9e4b0aab91c05fc69

Hunter, F. (2019). A student attended a protest at an Australian uni. Days later Chinese officials visited his family. *The Sydney Morning Herald*. Accessed 7.8.19. Retrieved from https://www.smh.com.au/politics/federal/this-student-attended-a-protest-at-an-australian-uni-days-later-chinese-officials-visited-his-family-20190807-p52eqb.html

Kuo, L. (2019). Hong Kong: three rallies mark 11th weekend of protests. *The Guardian*. Accessed 17.8.19. Retrieved from https://www.theguardian.com/world/2019/aug/17/hong-kong-three-rallies-mark-11th-weekend-of-protests

Lee, A., Li, F., & Kwan, S. (2019). As Many as Two Million Protesters Hit Hong Kong Streets. *Bloomberg*. Accessed 7.6.19. Retrieved from https://www.bloomberg.com/news/articles/2019-06-16/protests-swell-as-hong-kong-rejects-leader-s-compromise

Out in Hong Kong. (2019). Gay Games11 Hong Kong 2022. Accessed 7.8.19. Retrieved from https://www.gaygameshk2022.com/sign-4-support

Ma, N., & Cheung, E. (2019). *The Umbrella Movement: Civil Resistance and Contentious Space in Hong Kong*. Amsterdam: Amsterdam University Press.

Tomazin, F., & Zhuang, Y. (2019). Safe Schools scare campaign targets Chinese-Australian voters. *Sydney Morning Herald*. Retrieved from https://www.smh.com.au/federal-election-2019/safe-schools-scare-campaign-targets-chinese-australian-voters-20190427-p51hrk.html

Wolfe, N. (2019). 'That's a really embarrassing question': University of Queensland student lashes Tony Jones. *news.com.au*. Accessed 13.8.19. Retrieved from https://www.news.com.au/entertainment/tv/current-affairs/thats-a-really-embarrassing-question-university-of-queensland-student-lashes-tony-jones/news-story/164077a75bb42f3a64bc3ac9eda471b0

Jason Li is a pseudonym used by the author so they can freely discuss political issues. Jason is a student from Hong Kong, studying business in Australia. He currently lives with his boyfriend and his cat, and through living in this nation has developed a healthy respect for Australian spiders, snakes and swearing capacities. Whilst still in recovery from his first taste of Vegemite, 'Tim tam slams' have been a revelation.

FOUR IMAGES
JAKE CRUZ

168

OPPOSITE PAGE: PRINCESS. JAKE CRUZ

FAGGOT (L), FAIRY (R). JAKE CRUZ

Jake Alexander Cruz is an Australian illustrative artist whose works vastly explore homonormative experiences and contrasts them with the heteronormative structuring and values of societies both past and present, with an intent to expand on the variety of perspectives within the contemporary world. Cruz draws from his own experiences as a queer male and creates works focusing on how the body is perceived and how perceptions of his identity are read from his presentation.

FROOT LOOP. JAKE CRUZ

'SODOM TODAY, GOMORRAH THE WORLD!'
GEOFF ALLSHORN
Gay liberation and atheist liberation

In 2019, I attended a public event where speakers criticised the Australian government's proposed 'Religious Freedoms' Bills as a license to permit homophobic and transphobic discrimination. There, one prominent LGBTQIA+ community leader thanked 'queers of faith' for their ongoing work to defend LGBT rights—as well she should. And yet she failed to also thank queer non-believers, many of whom have also worked for queer rights. Perhaps she should have contemplated the words of heterosexual atheist Phillip Adams:

> There are some parallels here between atheism and homosexuality, 'the Love that dared not speak its name' as Oscar Wilde pronounced it, leading to millions living their life in the closet. Atheism was, and to a large extent still remains, the philosophy that dared not speak its name. And it's only recently that I've observed atheists coming out, finally confident enough—to borrow a gay slogan—to be loud and proud. Incidentally, spare a thought for gay atheists. (Adams, 2010, 2:37)

The concept of gay atheism is hardly a new idea: I have been living this reality for decades. Queer communities comprise individuals who have undertaken their own personal journey to arrive at a place of autonomy and empowerment, difference and diversity. Atheist communities are the same.

Losing my religion

I recall the exact moment when I realised that I had finally lost the last shreds of my religious world-view in the early 1990s. I was surrounded by my new, queer friends, at workshops for the AIDS Memorial Quilt, where people came in to make panels for those who had been lost to the epidemic. Together, we all shared cups of tea, shoulders to cry on, and lots of hugs. As a former Christian, I was momentarily dumbstruck to realise that there was more genuinely unconditional love in that room than in any church I had ever attended. This shell-shocked group of social outcasts, volunteer activists, and carers, taught me that treating others with basic love and respect was not the self-proclaimed monopoly of any one religion or philosophy, but was actually a pragmatic expression of our shared, common humanity.

And yet history tells a different story. It speaks of marginalisation and exclusion. Particularly under the historic influences of the Abrahamic religions, queers and atheists have been largely proscribed and persecuted: from the burning of witches, faggots and heretics, to family disinheritance and conversion therapy; from the execution of sodomites and apostates, to the ongoing cultural genocide of queer youth, and more.

I have previously noted Camille Beredjick's observation that religious homophobia can cause a queer person to become atheist (Allshorn, 2018, 116), and this is no more apparent than in the case of gay activist Sergeant Leonard Matlovich, a decorated Vietnam War veteran in the US Air Force. Coming out on the front cover of *Time* magazine in 1975, he was subsequently court-martialled and discharged by a panel of military personnel who were all religious (Duberman, 1991, 315). His Mormon church then excommunicated him, effectively not once but *twice*. Ultimately, 'his faith and spirituality were crushed and he considered himself somewhere 'between an agnostic and an atheist'.' (O'Donovan, 2004) His personal resilience and courage enabled his survival until his 1988 death from AIDS, but his loss of faith is rarely mentioned by biographers.

A similar case involves Henry Gerber, who founded the *Society for Human Rights*, which historian Jonathan Katz records as being the earliest documented gay rights organisation in the USA. Established in 1924, the Society was quickly targeted by police, who arrested its members and confiscated its documentation. This meant that both Henry Gerber and his Society—along with their altruistic ambitions— were largely erased from queer civil rights history. Gerber later attributed this fate, at least in part, to a mixture of 'religion and politics', self-identifying as 'now an avowed atheist' and openly espousing atheist views, such as: 'In America, where the Christian religion is losing ground, the horizon is growing brighter for homosexuals' (Katz, 1994, 419 & 554-557).

Such stories reflect an ongoing experience within our communities. When Israel Folau recently declared that gays and atheists (and other 'sinners') are going to hell, his was a familiar historical and cultural narrative regarding a purported hellish afterlife for people who are different—and a hell which many theists throughout history have seemed willing to create for us in this life as well.

'Smash the Church!'

The Stonewall riots and gay liberation are often proclaimed as being definitive moments in our fight for collective civil rights. But these were not explicitly the start of our collective queer journey out of oppression and towards liberation. Ultimately, this journey began whenever the first individual human being began to think independently and fight against his/her/their oppression. Thus we see the most basic parallel between queers and atheists.

Nor was this journey an easy one. Gay liberation was a war, a declaration of independence, and a call for social revolution. In the UK, the Gay Liberation Front (GLF) disrupted the 1971 launch of the Festival of Light (mudlark121, 2019). In the USA, one early GLF street slogan was: '2, 4, 6, 8, Smash the Church, Smash the State!' (Avicolli Mecca, 2009, back cover). *Daughters of Bilitis* co-founders Phyllis Lyon and Del Martin noted: 'Everything that's happened to oppress homosexuals today stems from organised religion. If it hadn't been for all that shit, we wouldn't have our problems today.' (Tobin & Wicker, 1972, 53-4) The 1971 Manifesto of the 'Third World Gay Revolution' stated: 'We want an end to all institutional religions because they aid in genocide by teaching superstition and hatred of Third World people, homosexuals and women...' (Jay and Young, 1992). One meme expressing such sentiment can be found on a Melbourne badge from that same era: *SODOM TODAY, GOMORRAH THE WORLD.*

In seeking to be all-encompassing, gay liberation created its own downfall. One GLF activist recalls: 'GLF didn't last. We got involved in these endless theoretical debates about what we should do and what our relationship was to other organisations... GLF disintegrated into so many splinter groups that it just disappeared' (Marcus, 1992, 185-6). In its wake, gay liberation seeded many other activist groups that shared its socially revolutionary aims, including some that subverted religious traditions. These included the Sisters of Perpetual Indulgence and the Radical Faeries.

This culture war continues today in other forms. Since losing the Marriage Equality postal survey, Australian religious right-wing conservatives have extended their attacks on the Safe Schools program and trans rights. They continue to advocate gay conversion therapy. They demand new 'religious rights' to discriminate against queer people. In our increasingly secular twenty-first century world, such religious bigotry provides a strong argument for atheism. It also demonstrates how inadequate are outdated dogmas to provide guidance in a future that may contain new understandings of life, habitat, self-identity, human rights, gender and sexuality. Humanity will surely find fresh perspective in the quote from JBS Haldane that the Universe is queerer than we can suppose.

The history of queer atheism is the story of striving to build such a future.

The rise and fall of militant gay atheism

A formal LGBT atheist movement was born during the ascendancy of gay liberation idealism in the 1970s. This was an era when 'Kill A Queer For Christ' bumper stickers adorned some US motor vehicles (Perry & Swicegood, 1991, 13) while anti-gay campaigns were led by US conservatives such as Anita Bryant and John Briggs. The anti-gay Briggs Initiative of 1978 was soundly defeated after US President Jimmy Carter publicly spoke against it, following a rally by gay atheist protesters at a public meeting (Rolfson, 1978a, 7). In his last column in the *Bay Area Reporter* before his assassination, gay atheist Harvey Milk credited gay atheist Tom Rolfsen with being instrumental in ensuring President Carter's public support: 'And Tom Rolfsen pulled it all together in Sacramento last week. Tom's idea, Tom's work, Tom's money, and a group went up there to confront the President of the United States. The rest is history. Congratulations Tom …' (cited in Rolfsen, 1978b, 5).

Rolfsen and his lifelong partner, Chal Cochran, became founding members of GALA (the Gay Atheist League of America, later renamed Gay And Lesbian Atheists), in 1976. Their San Francisco chapter ran social events and meetings, and published a monthly newsletter and various magazines. The *GALA Review* began publication in 1978 and continued until 1989, at which point it boasted over a thousand readers; however, the workload upon then-76 year-old Rolfsen forced a scaling-back of their activities (GALA Board, 1989, 1).

It is Texas where perhaps the most controversial gay atheist activities were led by gay couple Don Sanders and Mark Franceschini. The 'Houston LGBT History' web page is a good source of material regarding the social, activist, and outreach activities of this Houston group, and of the openly hostile reception it frequently received from religious members of their local community. Operating since 1981, the group began its decline in September 1992 following the death of 38 year-old Franceschini, whose obituary testified: 'From gay pride parades to ACT UP demonstrations, Mark Franceschini could be counted on to yell the loudest and walk the proudest' (Sanders, 1993, 4). His partner, Don Sanders, died three years later (Texas Obituary Project, 1995).

These atheist groups—once fueled by gay liberation anger and outrage—are now largely forgotten by queer historians and social commentators. A new generation appears to prefer a less confrontational form of atheist activism.

Humanism and human rights

Australian-born UK activist Peter Tatchell is one example of a gay atheist for modern times. He has been a prominent humanist and human rights activist for many years, and is director of the *Peter Tatchell Foundation*. He observes, 'A decent, better world is possible— and we don't need religion to make it happen. All we need is love and people willing to turn that love into political action for human freedom' (Tatchell, 2009, 309).

Another prominent example is someone who dates from the earliest days of queer rights. Gay activist pioneer, Magnus Hirschfeld, was a secular Jew, a humanist, and a socialist (*Tielman, 1997*). He co-founded the Scientific-Humanitarian Committee, which advocated for homosexual rights. He even joined the feminist movement because, as a gay man, he saw a link between the need for queer rights and women's rights (Finamore 2018).

Other overseas queer humanists have also been prominent activists. Antony Grey has been called 'Britain's first gay rights activist' after helping to secure law reform via the passage of the 1967 Sexual Offences Act (Geen 2010). Rob Tielman is credited with having played a 'prominent, pioneer role in the Dutch gay movement' (Gasenbeek and Gogineni 2002, 64), a movement which he documents as having existed continuously since 1911 (Tielman 1997, 21). Dan Savage is known for his writings and podcasts, and perhaps mostly for his 2010 founding of *It Gets Better*, an Internet website offering bullied GLBTIQ teenagers hope and positivity. Groups like the *LGBT Humanists UK*, the *Pink Triangle Trust* (UK), and the *LGBTQ Humanist Alliance* (USA), also enjoy a long history of activism.

Australia has its own proud history of humanist LGBT activism. In December 1966, the first issue of the *Australian Humanist (AH)* featured an article in which heterosexual women's rights activist Beatrice Faust supported gay rights (Faust, 1966, 2). Public meetings, networking, and other activism ensued. Subsequent discourse included gay activist Lex Watson writing subversively in the December 1971issue of *AH* that: 'Homosexuality is an alternative sex role, an alternative life style, as inconsequential in one sense as a preference for red hair to black.' (Watson, 1971, 38).

In 1970, the Humanist Society of Victoria produced a pamphlet entitled, *The Homosexual and the Law—A Humanist View*, and sent a copy to every member of State Parliament. Further copies sold out in bookshops, necessitating at least one reprint run (Reinganum, 1971, 6). The 5-page booklet criticised the law for its foundation in Biblical scripture, reinforced by its prohibition of what was legally termed 'the abominable crime of buggery'—an emotive word that prevented Australian society from adopting a more 'reasoned approach' to the issue (HSV, 1970, 1 & 2). The booklet was later reprinted by *Society Five*, an early Melbourne gay rights group (Society Five, 1974).

Humanism offers more than simply an atheist version of liberation theology. It provides ethical cogency for atheists, agnostics, secularists and the non-religious. Humanism proposes more than a negative attitude ('atheist' = 'non-theist') and provides opportunities to contribute positively to society.

Love thy neighbour

Lesbian atheist comedian Sue-Ann Post quips: 'I once auditioned for the part of Mary Magdalene in *Jesus Christ Superstar*. I gave what I thought was a very realistic rendition of, 'I Don't Know How To Love Him'.' (Post, 2010, 6:02) Levity aside, the problem of 'feeling the love' is very real in Australia, where I see religious privilege in our queer communities. I observe queer theists dominating public discourse and setting queer agendas, while openly atheist speakers are largely excluded from queer conferences, rallies, newspapers, publications, coalitions and networks. Only in independent social media discussions (and in *Bent Street*!) am I most likely to see any public acknowledgment that queer non-believers even exist.

Queer atheist blogger and author Greta Christina writes of similar experiences within US queer communities: 'I've heard LGBT leaders talk about how important it is to reach out to people of different religious faiths... with no mention whatsoever made of reaching out to people with no religious faith. Not even in lip service' (Christina,

2008). It must be questioned why queers cling so strongly to dying religious philosophies that have traditionally oppressed them.

Atheist liberation

While many religions claim a monopoly upon good works or virtue, the reality is that good people proliferate across space and time because of common humanity. Atheists are a part of this ubiquity. We can revisit the old GLF ideal of social transformation instead of assimilation, and use our difference to make a difference. This would surely marry the human existential desire for significance with a pragmatic, humanist response to the world's injustices.

In seeking to change the world, we should start with ourselves. Transphobic ideologies appear to have been adopted in some atheist circles (Sorrell, 2018; EssenceOfThought, 2019), demonstrating a need for queer atheists to participate in greater community discourse and thereby contribute to what gay atheist and HIV/AIDS activist Michael Callen advocated: 'The Healing Power of Love'.

Gay liberation may yet make way for atheist liberation—as exemplified in the life of US magician and atheist James Randi, who came out as gay in 2010 at the age of 81, stating on his website: 'Here is where I have chosen to stand and fight. And I think that I have already won this battle by simply publishing this statement' (Randi, 2010).

References

Phillip Adams, 2010. Speech at the *2010 Global Atheist Convention*, Melbourne; as recorded on DVD © Atheist Foundation of Australia & Atheist Alliance International, Siren Visual Australia & New Zealand.

Geoff Allshorn, 2018. 'A Case for Rainbow Atheism', in *Bent Street #2*, Melbourne: Clouds of Magellan Press, 115-119.

Tommi Avocolli Mecca, 2009. *Smash the Church, Smash the State! The Early Years of Gay Liberation*, San Francisco: City Light Books.

Greta Christina, 2008. 'How to be an Ally with Atheists', *Greta Christina's Blog*, 16 December. Accessed 23 July 2019, at https://gretachristina.typepad.com/greta_christinas_weblog/2008/12/how-to-be-an-ally-with-atheists.html

Martin Duberman, 1991. *About Time: Exploring the Gay Past*, New York: Penguin/Meridian Books.

EssenceOfThought, 2019. 'The Death Of The Atheist Community Of Austin—Testimonies From Volunteers & Service Users',

EssenceOfThought, 20 July; at https://m.youtube.com/watch?v=x0-yDOBDyuc

Beatrice Faust, 1966. 'Ethics and Morality', in *The Australian Humanist*, No. 1, December, 1—6.

Emma Finamore, 2018. 'Who Was Magnus Hirschfeld? Meet the Doctor and LGBT+ Activist Who Became A Nazi Target', *Pink News*, 17 April; at https://www.pinknews.co.uk/2018/04/17/who-was-magnus-hirschfeld-nazi-target-lgbt-activist-gay-rights-campaigner.

GALA Board, 1989. *GALA Realist*, October; at http://tinyurl.galegroup.com/tinyurl/BNvot2

Bert Gasenbeek and Babu Gogineni (eds.), 2002. *International Humanist and Ethical Union 1952-2002: Past, present and future*, Utrecht: De Tijdstroom uitgeverij,(IHEU ebook).

Jessica Geen, 2010. "First gay rights activist' Antony Grey dies aged 82', *Pink News*, 4 May; at http://www.pinknews.co.uk/2010/05/04/first-gay-rights-activist-antony-grey-dies-aged-82.

'Houston LGBT History' web page, at http://www.houstonlgbthistory.org/misc-atheists.html.

Humanist Society of Victoria, 1970. *The Homosexual and the Law—A Humanist View*.

Karla Jay and Allen Young (Eds.), 1992. Reprint of 'What We Want, What We Believe' from *Gay Flames* No.11, in *Out of the Closets: Voices of Gay Liberation*, twentieth anniversary edition, London: GMP Publishers, 363-367.

Jonathan Ned Katz, 1994. *Gay/Lesbian Almanac*, New York: Carroll and Graf Publishers.

Eric Marcus, 1992. 'The Radical Activist—Martha Shelley', in *Making History: The Struggle for Gay and Lesbian Rights*, New York: HarperCollins, 175-186.

mudlark121, 2019. 'Today in London religious history, 1971: the Gay Liberation Front mash up reactionary christian Festival of Light', Past Tense, 9 September; at https://pasttenseblog.wordpress.com/2019/09/09/today-in-london-religious-history-1971-the-gay-liberation-front-mash-up-reactionary-christian-festival-of-light/

Connell O'Donovan, 2004. 'Leonard Matlovich Makes Time', on *Affirmation:Gay & Lesbian Mormons* website, September. Retrieved from *Wayback Machine Internet Archive;* at https://web.archive.org/web/20090220032746/http://affirmation.org/memorial/leonard_matlovich_makes_time.shtml

Troy D Perry & Thomas LP Swicegood, 1991. *Profiles in Gay & Lesbian Courage*, New York: St Martin's Press.

Sue-Ann Post, 2010. Speech at the *2010 Global Atheist Convention*, Melbourne; as recorded on DVD © Atheist Foundation of Australia & Atheist Alliance International, Siren Visual Australia & New Zealand.

James Randi, 2010. 'How To Say It?', 21 March. *JREF Swift Blog*, James Randi
Educational Foundation; at
http://archive.randi.org/site/index.php/swift-blog/914-how-to-say-it.html

Carl Reinganum, 1971. 'Homosexual Law Reform Sub-Committee', in
Victorian Humanist, January, 6 & 7.

Thomas Rolfsen, 1978a. Editor. 'The Impossible Dream: The Sacramento
Story', *GALA Review* Issue 8, 2-7; at
http://tinyurl.galegroup.com/tinyurl/Atwj70

--------------------, 1978b. Editor. 'Harvey Milk: In His Own Words', *GALA
Review* Issue 9, 2-5; at http://tinyurl.galegroup.com/tinyurl/BNXXT8

Don Sanders, 1993. (Editor) 'Mark Franceschini', *The American Gay and
Lesbian Atheist*, Vol 10 Issue 9, AGA, September, 4; at
http://tinyurl.galegroup.com/tinyurl/APCY38

Society Five, 1974. *The Homosexual and the Law—A Humanist View.*

EJ Sorrell, 2018. 'Is There Room In Atheism For Trans People?', *Center for
Inquiry*, 15 June; at
https://centerforinquiry.org/blog/is_there_room_in_atheism_for_tr
ans_people/

Peter Tatchell, 2009. 'My Nonreligious Life: A Journey from Superstition to
Rationalism', in Russell Blackford & Udo Schüklenk (eds.), *50 Voices
of Disbelief: Why We Are Atheists*, West Sussex: Blackwell Publishing,
300-309.

Texas Obituary Project, 1995. 'Don Sanders', at
http://www.texasobituaryproject.org/052695sanders.html

Rob Tielman, 1997. 'Homosexual Rights: Why Humanism Cares', *Free Inquiry*,
Fall, Vol 17 No 4, 21 & 22.

Kaye Tobin and Randy Wicker, 1972. *The Gay Crusaders*, New York:
Paperback Library.

Lex Watson, 1971. 'But Would You Marry One?', *The Australian Humanist*,
No. 8, December, 36—38.

Geoff Allshorn is a former school teacher who has recently been undertaking postgraduate research on the history of HIV/AIDS. He has been a member of many LGBT and other community/activist groups, and has received a number of awards relating to this activism. He is also a former member of various atheist/humanist groups, and is currently the co-convenor of the Rainbow Atheists Facebook and MeetUp pages.

THE YEAR IN QUEER

In 2019 attacks on many other communities' human rights intensified in most locations, with shameless international interference from a variety of quarters exacerbating tensions for geopolitical gains. In response hyper-queer media and LGBTIQ activist cultures snapped back. Song, protest and legislative battles were used with an unapologetic, fabulous ferocity.

January

Randy Rainbow delivered 2019's US political news; queered… as hyper-camp musical parody that energised LGBTIQ activists. In January Rainbow had fans cry-laughing to 'The Donald Trump Cellblock Tango Part One'—aka, 'He had it coming' (https://m.youtube.com/watch?v=ihvgfU_g7LI).

By July the solo star so enslaved a grateful globe exhausted by US rights violations, Rainbow was nominated for an Emmy. Most episodes start with an impeccably preened, pink-tied and pink-bespectacled Rainbow 'interviewing' hilariously timed footage of a scandalised-Trump-hire-de-jour. Cue witty quips, facial contortions and liberal peppering of deadpan slang: 'yas qween', 'ok gurl', 'calm down' and 'ew'. Rainbow roars re-worded renditions of Madonna's Borderline on immigration injustice ('Border Lies'); Wizard of Oz numbers on the impeachment inquiry ('If You Only Got Impeached') or Oklahoma!'s title hit as a call for more secret recordings ('Omarosa!'). Fan faves included 'Cruella Devos'.

February

Education and Indigenous LGBTIQ activists were celebrating victories. France's Parliament voted to replace the gendered guardianship words in official school forms instead using terms which simply numbered a child's guardians (https://voiceofeurope.com/2019/02/france-changes-mother-and-father-to-parent-1-and-parent-2-under-new-law/). This legislation is designed to guarantee equal treatment for pupils with parents of the same sex but also to reflect the diverse realities of children's families and guardianship structures. New Jersey became the second US state to require public schools to teach LGBT and disability-inclusive material. In Australia Koori Gras was a celebration of Indigenous LGBTIQ+ diversity representation and performing arts—Jamie James' photography of this event is included in the this issue of Bent Street.

March

LGBTIQ+ advocacy to religious leaderships advanced relations to great effect. Evangelical churches in Austria and Germany—countries which recently legalised same sex marriage—started turning the tide in their treatment of LGBTIQ people by allowing blessings of same-sex marriages. Austria's Evangelical Church of the Augsburg Confession kicked off the move (https://kurier.at/chronik/oesterreich/evangelische-synode-will-homosexueller-paare-oeffentlich-segnen/400430599) followed by the Reformed Church and later Germany's Evangelical-Lutheran Church in Württemberg. Throughout the year the Evangelical-Lutheran Church of Hanover, Evangelical Church of the Palatinate, German reformed Church of Lippe, UK Methodist Church, Evangelical Reformed Church of the Canton of Zürich, Swiss Reformed Church, Reformed Church of Aargau and Evangelical Reformed Church of Northern Germany joined the movement and shifted their approach.

April

Rights battles in the Asia Pacific benefited from inquiries by global rights bodies ensuring rights accountabilities through UN civil society bodies and regional courts. Brunei tried to introduce the stoning to death of gay people (https://www.google.com.au/amp/s/www.bbc.com/news/amp/wor

ld-asia-47769964) only to back pedal in May under huge international
pressure. United Nations inquiries into rights in the region had at least
some effect: homosexuality was instead criminalised without capital
punishment, and lesbianism fined.

May

Todrick Hall self-released 2019's much-needed fortifying pride
anthem 'Nails Hair Hips Heels'

(https://m.youtube.com/watch?v=TQ04gPb4LlY). From the very
first moment the strong slinky singer sashays sharply through a giant
neon pink triangle; this unapologetic song demanded respect and
snapped its fingers in the faces of those refusing it. Hall struts into a
factory full of glam, gloved, high heeled men. A former Ru Paul's
Drag Race contestant, Hall brings 'Paris is Burning' legendary levels
of competitive commitment to dragtastic ball-culture catchphrases,
finger flicks and facial expressions whilst sassing:

'I don't dance I work (work), I don't play I slay (slay),
I don't walk I strut (strut), strut and then sashay (okay).'

The video teaches iconic vogues: throwing 'shade' whilst saying 'girl'
and kicking a 'shablam' to the ground, heels in air, fan flapping in a
downpour of glitter. Generously for those who can't shablam,
blinking is made a 'dance move'. Hall's 'Haus Party' hits 'I Like Boys'
and 'Glitter' were a fierce reclaiming of queer strength.

June

African LGBTIQ+ rights activists such as Kat Kai Kol-Kes have been battling the criminalising influence of US evangelical interventions into their legal status with some success in courts. Kat Kai Kol-Kes and a sea of peers raised a rainbow flag outside the High Court of Botswana when it unanimously decriminalised both female and male same-sex sexual acts on June 11th (https://edition-m.cnn.com/2019/06/11/africa/botswana-lgbtq-ruling-intl/index.html?r=https%3A%2F%2Fen.m.wikipedia.org%2F). Evangelising organisations like the World Congress of Families continue to try to infiltrate African nations and promote legislation against African LGBTIQ citizens, with various groups setting their sights on returning Uganda's Kill the Gays Bill or agitations in Jamaica and Ghana. Pan-African and global collaborative aid is needed to shield African LGBTIQ and reinforce resilience in this brave, bitter battle for their lives.

July

Vigorous efforts to ensure LGBTIQ+ representation peopling Polish pride matches and street protests fought the **use of** 'LGBT-free Zone' stickers in Warsaw. The Warsaw district court ordered that the Gazeta Polska's distribution of these discriminatory anti-LGBT stickers should halt pending the resolution of a court case (https://www.hrw.org/news/2019/08/01/polish-court-rebukes-lgbt-free-zone-stickers). However the editor of the Gazeta Polska dismissed the ruling using the claim it was 'fake news' and censorship, and that the paper would continue distributing decals with a modified version of the slogan 'LGBT Ideology-Free Zone'. This effort appears reminiscent of other media and social media based international intervention efforts aimed at inciting division in, and thus weakening, nations surrounding Russia.

August

Tamil Nadu became the first state in India to ban enforced medically unnecessary surgical intervention on infants and children with intersex variations, with an exception of cases where it would be required to overcome life-threatening situations (https://www.thehindu.com/news/national/tamil-nadu/tn-bans-sex-reassignment-surgeries-on-intersex-infants-

children/article29273674.ece). The Madras High Court Justice GR
Swaminathan had directed India's Tamil Nadu Government to issue
the Government Order banning enforced medically unnecessary
surgeries on infants and children with intersex variations back in May
(https://www.thenewsminute.com/article/ban-sex-reassignment-
surgeries-intersex-infants-madras-hc-tells-tn-govt-100565).

October

Australia's Community Action for Rainbow Rights (CARR) Protesters
converged at Town Hall on October 12.
(http://www.starobserver.com.au/news/national-news/new-south-
wales-news/sydney-marches-against-religious-discrimination-bill-
tomorrow/188072). They gathered with signs and loud speakers to
protest the government's Religious Discrimination Bill package
(including three separate texts announced earlier in the year by the
Attorney General). The rainbow crowd marched through the CBD to
prevent health professionals and education providers being given the
right to refuse services everyone has a right to, on grounds of
religious belief. The bills would also enshrine existing powers for
religious schools to sack or expel LGBTQI teachers and students and
grant new rights to discriminate for religious charities.

As the year wraps up, its forwards-backwards-forwards battles for LGBTIQ
human rights recognition, religious support, safety, media and creative
visibility continue. They are injected with an additional energy from the
inspirations of not only a new wave of hyper-queer LGBTIQ media, but the
relentlessness of LGBTIQ advocates in intersecting climate change and
democratic freedom movements surging into the world from Sweden and
Hong Kong. Advocates are taking on odds that only 'seem' impossible, by
first envisioning and then pursuing more positive possibilities.

POETRY

RENOVATOR'S DELIGHT
Terry Jaensch

*Perfect for a first home buyer, investor or even someone wanting
to develop. **

3 hairline fractures in right wrist; swing, horse
shower: as per concession to form not
listed chronologically. the lot,
teeth that is, braced twice, a matter of course

at 13, a matter off course again
at 21. gums, a kind of cancer
at … needles, novocaine … can't remember
age, just the scalpel's blade, arresting. then

somewhere in there, between the horse & swing —
reversed here for variant rhyme — the nose
cauterized. & a fresh gall bladder-ing

save that, intact inside; though i suppose
i took the nurse at his word — on waking.
make a home of me? *take me at mine. Close.

EXT. PARK. NIGHT.
Terry Jaensch

Meeting again like this at a beat is, to say the least, unexpected —
we're tripping over ourselves to catch up. We look the same,
our shared lack of embarrassment equates to a kind of twin-ship.
Only our heights effect a separation. Our imperfect Janus-head
turned from the fortress' gates establishes as fact our resistance
to attack. Not having warred for the best part of a decade — we've
lost the facility to war. The only gun in our arsenal an unerring
sense of fashion. How is it possible we've dressed for the occasion?
The plaid nostalgia of my suit, the faux stance of your designer fatigues,
even my glasses, tinted rose pink, seem to say peace. Possums grip
the lip of a bin's smacked gob, pull from detritus the composed core
of an apple. We ask the easy questions first — work, study — each
ascended path achieving the same kudos lit plain. Tourists lag
scorched offerings in hand. Shadows do emerge, but not ours,
we cannot be coerced — our branches teeming. We maintain
a distance whispering. Our talk indiscreet here, everything
but sex. Incidentally, that's how we began.

Terry Jaensch is the author of three books of poetry: *Buoy* (Five Islands Press), *Excess Baggage & Claim* co-authored with Singaporean poet Cyril Wong (Transit Lounge Publishing) and *Shark* (Transit Lounge Publishing).

BIRDS THAT HAUNT ME

Ashley Williams

I
George Lane Mandarin Duck

My uncle's mandarin duck lost its single ovary,
shed the bland brown plumes of subdued femininity and
donned a masculine orange, white and emerald sail.

He said I am like this duck. Or like a maned lioness,
with my deep throaty voice and my broad puffed-out chest.
He says I need my hormones fixed; and so I tell him he's the quack.

II
Lygon Street Lark

My gleeful cheers
For the lovely lark I imagined was
 Just hovering in 'hello'
Near my girlfriend's shoulder
'Like in Snow White, oh look!'
With *a smile and a song*
I sang the soundtrack
To its abrupt beak piercing
The white of her eye,
Her 'sclera'

The sclera structures the eye
helps it

keeP sh
ApE
We learned, when hers
didn't
AnymO
rE … whA t
A laR k.

III
Queen's Road Quaker Monk Parrot

'Beep, beep beeeeeeep'
'It's time darling'
'It's time, get up'

'Must you tweet this early?'
'Twitter isn't life.'
'There's no secrets online'.

'Cup of tea?'
'Cup of tea?'
'Cup of tea?'
'Ooh yes my darling!'

'Tell me your secret!'
'You'll tell the bird!'
'You'll tell the bird!'
'The bird tells everyone!'

'Stop your henpeckin''

'Cup of tea?'
'Cup of tea?'
'Cup of tea?'
'Ooh yes my darling!'

'Tweety-tweet'
'You tweet better than Trump'
'Tweety-tweet'
'Chirping away'
'Stop your henpeckin''
'Chirping away'
'A couple of old birds'

Ashley Williams lives in Adelaide with their girlfriend and enjoys poetry, any-coloured wine and creepy looking cheeses. Ashley has written experimentally for a few years and was inspired by past Bent Street poets to contribute some of their work.

CREEK
Michelle Bishop

Putrid, stinking waterways,
breeding rubbish and muck –
visible as I cross the bridge.
Cars race by. One driver,
no passengers.
Roots protrude from concrete homes,
asphyxiated by fumes.
These life-givers are choking to death.
Leaves and branches and trunks
turn grey under the weight of poison.
Flaccid and forgotten.
We converge like cattle at the lights,
waiting for the (green) man to dictate
our safe passage.
Foot tapping and deep sighs
resounding. Energy screaming
hurry! I'm busy! I shouldn't have to wait!
Twisted bellies bellow.
The light changes and
it's on—quick steps secure the lead,
dashing the six lanes of waiting traffic,
eyes averted from the lone driver tapping on the wheel,
energy screaming
hurry! I'm busy! I shouldn't have to wait!
Is this 'civilised'?

Michelle Bishop is a Gamilaroi woman who was grown up on Dharawal Country where she lives with her partner. She is currently an Associate Lecturer in the Department of Educational Studies at Macquarie University and is completing a PhD which envisions Indigenous education sovereignty.

SAMUEL LUKE BEATTY
COMFORTABLE

COMFORTABLE (following pages) was created for Read To Me (at Knox Street Bar, Chippendale, NSW) and read in front of a live audience (on May 7, 2019). This autobiographical comic (four frames are reprinted here) was created from journal entries Samuel wrote to process some of his complicated feelings and emotions about being one year on testosterone, over 7 months post-op top surgery, yet still feeling uncomfortable in his body. It is an intimate look into his trans experience, sharing vulnerabilities about body image, childhood memories of gender, socialisation, and navigating the world as a trans person.

Comfortable—the full sequence—can be viewed online at samuellukeart.com

FOLLOWING PAGES: FROM 'COMFORTABLE'. SAMUEL LUKE BEATTY

I STILL OCCUPY MY BODY AND NAVIGATE THE WORLD IN MY MINDS-EYE OF HOW I USED TO LOOK AND HOW I USED TO SOUND PRE-TRANSITION.
LIKE A SHADOW THAT I CAN'T SHAKE.
IN THAT DISTRESSED MINDSET THAT PEOPLE ARE STILL STARING AT ME. TRYING TO FIGURE OUT WHETHER I'M A GIRL OR A BOY. AND IN SPENDING SO MANY YEARS MAKING MY BODY INVISIBLE FROM MYSELF AND FROM OTHERS, I BECAME COMFORTABLE WITH FEELING UNCOMFORTABLE. AND NOW I'M SPENDING MY TIME HEALING FROM THAT INTERNALISED TRAUMA. AND LEARNING HOW TO BE VISIBLE AGAIN.

IT'S ALARMING HOW LONG THE MIND CAN TAKE TO CATCH UP TO YOUR BODY, EVEN WHEN YOU KNOW YOU CAN BE COMFORTABLE NOW. THAT YOU CAN BREATHE NOW. THAT THERE ARE NO MORE CHEST BINDERS. THAT THE FIGHT IS OVER. THAT I'VE DONE THE BIGGEST, MOST LIFE-CHANGING THINGS THAT I'LL PROBABLY EVER DO IN MY LIFE.

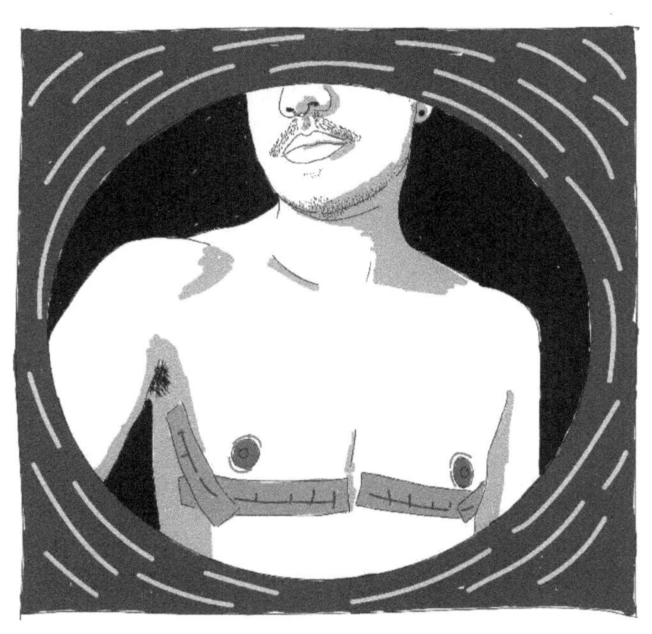

BUT I NEED TO RE-LEARN
HOW TO OCCUPY MY OWN
BODY. AND I NEED TO
RE-LEARN HOW TO BE
COMFORTABLE IN IT.

I'D ALWAYS STRUGGLED WITH BODY
DYSPHORIA BEFORE I KNEW WHAT
GENDER DYSPHORIA WAS, OR WHAT
BEING TRANSGENDER MEANT TO ME.
I WAS ALWAYS HYPERAWARE OF
FEELING OUT OF PLACE IN MY BODY.
NOT FEELING CONNECTED TO THE
SPACE I OCCUPIED. OR THE
VESSEL THAT WAS MEANT TO
REPRESENT ME.

COLOUR'S END
Xavier

Green's end

It costs one truth to join this hellion
Unite right now in saving Mother Earth
Live life in extinction rebellion

Be a firey Circumcellion
Without promising after-life rebirth
It costs one truth to join this hellion

Our fathers are Machiavellian
Only increasing their bank accounts' girth
Live life in extinction rebellion

They cannot buy air with their billion
Bridal and pride marches offer no mirth
It costs one truth to join this hellion

Their own greed is buying and selling them
Turning them into their own carbon's serf
Live life in extinction rebellion

Kick coal power like a triskelion
Legislate the land like you know its worth
It costs one truth to join this hellion
Live life in extinction rebellion

Rainbow's end

Golden toupee
Golden sire
Golden tan spray
Golden liar

Golden gowns by
Golden sashes
Golden crowns buy
Golden pashes

Golden wives and
Golden daughters
Golden lives span
Golden borders

Golden gabbing
Golden pushy
Golden grabbing
Golden pussy

Golden bawdry
Golden tower
Golden laundry
Golden shower

Golden pickle
Golden camera
Golden sickle
Golden hammer

Black's end

If poems should be the best words
inked in the best order and
politicians the best people
hired in the best jobs then
I can't make rhyme nor
reason of them

They tip and drip all ink from the page, cleansing
the black from the white

Closing their immigration borders
their gender borders
their eyes
our legs, but not
their mouths

Until the page is only
white

Xavier describes himself as a Black Australian poet and first year university student, not out to family. The inspirations for his work include: joining the 'Extinction Rebellion' protests to push for recognition of the climate emergency (https://rebellion.earth/), his frustrations with governments and particular policies, and gaps in generational awareness of the issues younger generations face.

cab thoughts: EMP ty
Anna Leah D. Luna-Raven

thank you yell-OWWW taxi!

thank you play on words.
thank you afterthought.
here i am on my way home.
on my way back.
and here i am.
on my way to thinking about you.
catching myself before i completely do.
thank you.
for the temporary calm.
for the (temporary) respite.
for this temporary cave.
from the maddening world
from this crazy world.
temporary though, i say,
for i know for a fact that
there will come a time
when they will find you.
find out about you.
am not supposed to put this into writing
for fear that they might use this to find you
but still decided to do so
lest i myself forget.
about you.
this is a reprise of the denouement.
over and again.
never ends does it?
thank you my big.
thank you song.
thank you premonition.
thank you no. 25.
thank you paris.
thank you for curbing your enthusiasm.
and your pain.
and everything else.

would you like to hear about mine?
thank you for the unexplained silence.
thank you bruno.
have you gotten yours yet?
thank you long wait.
the other shoe fell.
the loose tooth fell off.
thank you, my heart did drop too.
thud, it said.
thank you broken heart --- OWWW.
and still having to owe.
thank you unfair trade.
you said so yourself.
after all, you can't always get a free ride.
thank you what-not.
trying to make a big decision.
with the meter running, thank you.
thank you limit.
thank you for the ride.

this is me.
getting off now.
keep the change.

Anna Leah D. Luna Raven is a straight ally who recently lost one of her gay best friends to lymphoma. Her queer supporters loved her poems and other writing, and so do we. *Bent Street* welcomes our allies' and accomplices' submissions.

TRADING SAINTS
Jocelyn Deane

Devotion(s)

Say we're sat cross legged, however
many of us, arms twinned
watching Lizzie McGuire re-runs,
where she has her first kiss, and
her heart broken when Ronnie says later
– we all repeat
we need to talk, in different voices.
You are impersonating
Ronnie deliciously: the small fry
of recurring pubescence, the seriousness
ejected into velar consonants, the thawing pause
before 'Lizzie …' which lasts as long as
he desires. Lizzie and he interact
only that one episode; he likes a girl at a distant
New York school, and says he doesn't know if now
is the time for he and Lizzie to stay exclusively boyfriend and
girlfriend.
Ronnie is
a paper-route in the mid 2000's
like Clark Kent
not making sense to work at a print newspaper
in 2019.
We are trading our tertiary characteristics
like playing D&D; we grip one
another and
compliment Hillary Duff on her diamond smile
and endless patience with ciscum and lie one on top of
the other like newly-born kittens developing
eyes, very still.

Eating Jesus

Jesus tasted so

Good: all umami

Multitudes enfolded

In a meat-loaf one

Devoured with big

Faces—shark-wide—

Saying—'This

Is ours now. Thou

art a whale, Oh

Man …

– A profit of deep space sheltering

      nothing before you

Beheld …' his huge palms

spread. Converging, we make

black pudding of his blood,

distributed through our farmers markets,

unbuttoned
– tender—his chest

with our teeth, sticky and red,

fraught with roses

under a skinny loam.

– Take, eat—we mouth

lips,

Our middle and forefinger spelling

A smile on dark beard-line with

Braille delicacy—This:

Is my body Give freely

It mouths licking away

The too heavy stone

of him the peach

that passeth

not

Trading Cards

You suggest playing Pokémon
cards with the saints, their diversity
and collectible-wide range
passing dry winters in Coyoacán,
a street musician's distance
from a plaster, huge Christ-child,
ice-blue, genitalia revealed.
Play in the patio we recognise is keeping more
specific names, like shiny Blastoises, debating baroque
and gothic architecture, virtues as
– if buildings unearth and
make pilgrimage to each other over
continents. The Cathedral Metropolitana was
built on the Tenochtitlan Templo Mayor
you say; sacrifices are necessary
to keep the sun alive and
the sky bluish. The Spanish hardly understood
when they exhumed the bodies, succulent as
stakes in the earth. Play
Pokémon cards with the saints in Coyoacán,
using a thunder-stone to turn your saint Sebastian
– yellow from love—
into a Raichu.

Jocelyn Deane (they/them) was born in the UK, in 1993, and moved to
Australia in 2001. They study linguistics at Unimelb and work as a
disability representative at the student union. Their work has appeared in
Cordite, *Australian Poetry* and *Seizure mag*, among others. In 2013 they
were one of the recipients of the 457 Visa prize for poetry, and in 2015
was shortlisted for the Marsden and Hachette Young Writers award.
'Devotions' and 'Eating Jesus' are new creations and 'Trading Cards' first
appeared in the Transqueer edition of *Cordite* magazine in 2018.

HER HOMOPHOBIC HUSBANDS
Reese Downing

Her Husband #1
Praised did not so much want her
as he wanted someone
he could mould

It helped that she wasn't quite
formed yet and her clay was
still not cold

Praised banned her from visiting
– without him!—the house of
her best friend

He set Qu'ran passages
for her to recite by
each week's end

She read 'ye are a people
who exceed' And then she
spat out '*Girls*'.

I read 'young boys of their own',
And snorted 'as fair as
virgin pearls'.

Her Husband #2
Peter Peter didn't eat her
Had a wife and couldn't keep her
satisfied
He never tried
And so, of course, it died

Peter Peter spineless cheater
Victim blamer poofter beater
and admirer
Man desirer
His punch was a liar

Her Husband #3
Pastors like Paul
wear wide brimmed Kmart hats
as they clip her lawns
She yawns
but forgets me
She'd never let me
attend their smug barbeques
that stretch for hours like sermons
She sours
but pretends to sweeten
as he rubs her feet and
listens to their daughters' news

Reese Downing is a bisexual poet.

GREETING CARD 3. ASHLEY SIEVWRIGHT

TWO POEMS
Stuart Barnes

Rainbow+ Rondeau

Everything is queer: the red-tailed skink
that ends its rear, the strong orange ink
of Malherbe's parakeet, the yellow
-mouthed Laysan albatross' green shadow
that at times appears blue as a rink;

the anglerfish's violet slink,
the black-spotted pond frog pleased to sink
the Japanese tree frog's brown shōmyō
('Everything Is Queer');

the hot spring-bathing snow monkey's pink
face, the unnamed white octopus' wink
at the unnamed grey one, the hollow
cyan blooms that coat the flamingo
that also scoops the mauve shrimp that sync
'Everything' 'Is' 'Queer'.

DVO

A dozen red rum and cola cans
then he enfolds my head like Ted Bundy.
'I love you, I'm the only one for you.'
His five o'clock shadow grazes my jugular

then he cajoles me into bed like Ted Bundy.
Migraine medication knocks me sideways.
Five o'clock, shadows graze on my jugular.
I said 'I'm sick.' I turn on the bedside lamp,

migraine medication knocks me sideways,
like smack. 'Hell d'you think *you're* goin?' 'Home.
I'm sick of this.' He upturns the bedside lamp
He's going crazy He tries to pick me up

then **SMACK!** 'No way in Hell you're goin home …
I'll drive off a cliff into the sea,' he screams.
He tried to pick me up I'm going crazy
Pick me up I text from the hotel's locked bathroom.

*

He screamed I'll drive off a cliff into the sea
—OCD's re-established its octopus grip—
I texted pick me up from the hotel's locked bathroom
I google harassment self-defence intruder

OCD's re-established its octopus grip.
Nightly, his black V8 gulps my air.
I google harassment self-defence intruder
I procure an aluminum alloy baseball bat.

Black, I gulp solitaire and V8 daily.
The order's granted eight months from our blind date.
I obscure the aluminum alloy baseball bat.
I dream, I dream about a convoy of destroyers.

Eight months since our blind date, order's not granted.
'I love you, I'm the only one for you'
I dream. I dream about a convoy of destroyers:
a dozen red rum and cola cans.

Stuart Barnes' first book, *Glasshouses* (UQP), won the Arts Queensland
Thomas Shapcott Poetry Prize, was commended for the Anne Elder Award
and shortlisted for the Dame Mary Gilmore Award. From 2013-2017
Stuart was poetry editor of *Tincture Journal*, since 2017 he has been a
program advisor for the Queensland Poetry Festival. Stuart is working on
his second poetry collection, *Form & Function*, and a novel. 'DVO' was first
published in *Southerly Journal* 78.3 Violence

stuartabarnes.wordpress.com

#CBD
Adele Tan

What am I
      To you
or to me
or to him
or to her
or to them
Am I loved
or lovable
Do I love well enough
Do I hold well enough
Do I challenge enough
Without being challenging
Us vs them or
      Us and?
Will I be allowed to be part
      of your us

Adele, a Teochew woman, having worked in human rights as part of the community and arts sectors, is challenging herself to be more visible as a multicultural LGBTQIA+ community member with disability and chronic illness who is continuing an often difficult journey of transforming complex traumas including assault and domestic violence, into advocacy for social change. She is grateful to have been welcomed onto Noongar Boodjar. This poem comes from researching the origins of Celebrate Bisexuality Day and conversations with other bi/pan community members about the tensions of identity, celebration, community, activism and advocacy, and specifically the visibility and inclusion of bisexuality within the broader queer community, whilst maintaining emotional and psychological safety.

FICTION
Sleepy
Lagoon
MOTEL
VACANCY

ROAD ODE
CAT COTSELL

The wheels are part of my body. My circulation is maintained by a humming engine. I am carried in his ribs and I feel his vibrations in mine.

There is a transcendent immediacy in this state that exists nowhere else. My mind is empty, it is full. Every response is instinctive to lanes and curves, dips and hills. I have digitigrade legs. The clutch is my ankle, from the pressure plate through to the flywheel form the ball of my foot. My right foot presses gently on the accelerator and the brake, the same way my toes press on each other when it is cold. I am not driving. I am running.

I love driving alone. The highway could be a road to nothing in the middle of nowhere. It could be the line between heaven and earth. I have driven through underworlds, chthonic deities striding alongside us in the spacious dark of midnight, glancing at us with every fleeting flash of the headlights in the eyes of wild rabbits. In the day, I tilt my head back a little ways and we are in the sky, flying toward the cumulus rising from the horizon, fish belly monochrome in the fluorescent afternoon.

I have sat swathed in that dry crusty dust-oil-petrol smell, that love song aroma, surrounded by the rat-a-tat-tat pounding of the rain as the glass slowly fogs the grey landscape into an opaque and glistening silver, and felt—like belief—that the outside world was only a void.

*

Darby is a Corolla, a manual sedan born in 1995. Only four years younger than me. Four cylinders, four doors—the number *four* follows him around with mathematical superstition. He is 54 inches tall, faded and stout with grainy floor mats and shy flat headlights and two different wheel brands, and he is the most beloved car in the world.

I know by feel how far he needs to travel before his water or oil need topping up. When feeding him petrol, I know when to let go of the pump's trigger before it clicks. I know his turning circle with the same precision that I know the reach of my arm.

216

Darby was never 'mine'. If he is an extension of me, then he is my skin and hair and fingernails. Perhaps his attachment to me is flimsy in the grand scheme of things, but he is there, like a cat or a very old tree is 'there'.

*

We are beyond all of society and humanity. The anonymous highway, vast as a universe, is broken occasionally by a passing stranger. I wonder as I listen to the asphalt roar if they feel what I am feeling. On the way towards and from, how many people frantically apologise to the steering wheel after jarring over a speed bump or after grinding their gears? How many stalled, and felt it in their throat like a choke? On the highways and craggy dirt roads, how many of them patted their dashboard for no particular reason and said *good baby*?

It is surreal to drive through a quiet unfamiliar town, only learning its name as I pass the sign, a town with its own school and its own fish'n'chip shops, and think: *this is someone's home.* Someone's static, someone's comfortingly boring origin. And my own hometown feels just as mysterious to another stranger. I look through the windshield as an alien looking through the viewer on their shuttlecraft, arriving on earth for the first time. Civilisation is only familiar for being civilisation. Darby travels through too fast to let me imagine that this stranger's hometown, this cluster of life, is more known to me than it really is.

*

Darby was not originally my car. Mum bought him for cheap from a guy with six cars in his backyard, for my brother. At first he was going to pick up Darby, then he was going to pay mum back first, then he was just a bit behind.

Disorganisation is our family's inheritance.

Darby lived with me like a stray dog for months, until I adopted him, and he became mine. My brother was not disappointed. We are putter-offers, and if a problem solves itself or becomes someone else's, it is usually considered a success.

I was renting with strangers in an unsecure house and was struggling. I was in, what I told people, a *weird place*. Darby and I shared directionless-ness. We had both been left behind by someone, and were battling along as if we had not noticed being left behind.

Sometimes on long drives I would roll down the window to let the noise in. From inside his body Darby teemed with disgruntled little tremors, but from outside he roared. I liked having my ear pressed to his chest, hearing his thrumming humming heartbeat, but it was satisfying to hear wheels bellowing along bitumen.

*

He broke down on the Tuggeranong parkway. I was on the way to meet some friends. Due to a minor problem, I had to wait three hours before NRMA could send someone out. We sat at the side of the road, he and me, feeling other cars fly past.

Rust had gotten in deep, deep down in his old mechanical organs. Darby was beyond the reach of mechanics or auto shops or skilled uncles. He had to be towed. The wait for the tow-truck was shorter, and longer, than the wait for help.

*

I wonder every time I get behind the wheel if I'll be disappointed when I reach where I'm going. I never am. This simple feeling is the only pure joy I have ever found in the world. Nothing about it is unpleasant, not even the end.

When I die, I think, if heaven exists, this is what mine will be. Not a destination. A road for a home, a faded steel chassis for a body, and the incomparable peace of the love of a car.

Cat Cotsell is a nonbinary panromantic creative based in Canberra. They recently graduated from UC with a Bachelor of Writing and Honours in Art & Design, and are currently building their portfolio. Their short fiction and poetry can be found on FIVE:2:ONE, Everyday Fiction and Indolent Book's *What Rough Beast* project. They also illustrate under the name Cat Hesarose.

THE ARRANGEMENT
HENRY VON DOUSSA

If it had occurred online, you'd have called it catfishing. He gave little of himself away, almost nothing. I prompted, he resisted, arguing it would be his essence, not his details, I would come to know, and, as I suspect he had already calculated, would come to need.

Initially, he sold himself as a thirty-something bisexual in a relationship with a woman. She was away on business, he quickly added, a small nugget of detail to ground and enrich his first lie. Bisexuality it seemed had a currency he thought lent him a desirability and toughness to match the black tracksuit pants and black hoodie he wore for cruising, garments which further hid the reality of his undisclosed past, as well as the depth of the wrinkles around his electric eyes and exactly where the retreat of his hairline was up to.

When I first saw him holding court amongst the men, I was enchanted. We met only at night but flowers bloomed and swayed. Seedpods opened even though it was winter, and hoped, as I hoped, that in the seeding desire would take hold. Forget-me-nots, benign and gentle in their soft blue colouring, cunningly attached themselves to my socks to be sure the enchantment would spread, sprout and then lace itself in places it had no right to exist; in a different life I had elsewhere. The pods needled themselves to my pants to be taken home as small gifts to remember the occasion, a bomboniere of sorts. I found one of the sticky little buggers in my wallet and another under my pillow when I was making the bed and fluffing the cushions.

Chrysanthemums too, I saw from the corner of my eye as I scanned about for danger; the flowers you give on Mother's Day. The flowers we gave our beloved but dishevelled mother to acknowledge another year of her sentence and servitude passing, not reducing, but passing because she knows, don't we all, that the mess she has lovingly created, nurtured and left to repeat itself will outlive her. To top it off, the fragrance of wattle pollen got up my nose as the tiny spores whose individuality is easily lost but collectively shines brightly in yellow bursts, swirled about in the wind. The pollen left with me too on dirty jeans with sodden knees and crumpled cuffs to be discretely washed off in the trough on laundry night, the night after the bins go out and the night before we shop and vacuum the house.

Masterfully, he choreographed the four or five men among the flowers—a leg here, an arm there, 'You on your knees'. Moving one man behind another, 'that's how he likes it,' he whispered into the ear of the man still on his feet, all the while removing none of the black wrap that concealed him. He too was creating a posy, an odd collection of flowers that would usually not go together: soft and hard stems, annuals and perennials, indigenous and colonising petals. In the same way a posy is put together by a florist, stems stripped of outer leaves before being crosshatched at various degrees to avoid the blooms on top, the most coveted part, being crushed together and the individual beauty of each bloom drowned out or bruised by the others around it. To prevent this, and to see each man shine, he slid some men in on an angle.

Ultimately, as with all posies, the group was tied tightly; tied together with the relief of finding each other and of not being exiled to the uninvited men who watched on; bound twice and tied with a knot as firm and hopeful as 'I will'. All this done, he would have said, 'Without getting my hands dirty'. He was not lazy, but had honed his craft for maximum effect with the smallest effort. His use of cleverly placed words was no different. Calculated. Sparse. Effective. When other men might have simply appropriated a mundane and safe script, saying in gravelly tones, 'You're hot', he, while pushing me forward, leant into my ear and said softly—said for me only—'You're dreamy, bitch, move'. And I did as I was told. He wore his confidence and bravado like medals as he rallied the troops.

In the positioning and repositioning, he moved me the most. I was where his attention fell. But I was not the centre. His desire was the centre. At most, I was a necessarily malleable part of what framed and contained it, what made it count for something. I searched about for how I might make myself matter and responded as required. I investigated him to find where I might be but very little was reflected back. In the *Lover's Discourse*, Roland Barthes places the endeavour of dismembering a lover's body in the hope of discovering what desire is in the same order of futility as a child dismantling a clock in the hope of discovering the origins of time. There was nothing until much later that I could dismantle for clarity. I may have had spit on my hands because every time I almost grasped my use to him or why I returned, any rationality for me saying yes, slipped away.

When the men slowly disappeared and it was just him and me and the various puddles of men's needs on the ground around us, he stroked my hair. With me on my knees and him standing over me, he stroked my hair and touched my face, 'Just relax, babe, just relax'. I looked up at his triumphant face. The pleasure in the men he had pulled together and what he had made happen, while obscured by the shadows cast from the edges of his hoodie, was obvious on his unshaven mask. He was pleased with himself. My need and hope grew further, and in the swirl of desire, I glimpsed Hannibal Lector. At the time, I did not consider this worth noting. All I saw was this cunning brute there for me. Later, I began to realise that like Dr Lector, he was the type of person who could talk a man into swallowing his own tongue. I looked up and saw that essence.

♋

Have I given you enough? Is an establishing shot required? Is this taking place outside, in a bedroom (they too can bloom with fields of flowers), by the sea or in the high country where the men would have dropped sawdust from their jeans as they slipped them past their knees? Is it a time when police routinely drove to the places homosexuals gathered to rough them up—and perhaps why our nameless fisher has concocted his disguise? Or a time after gays have been legitimised through marriage, so newly sanitised sexual morals could foster a different motivation to lie? Does the lens of my telling need to draw back for context?

I have been accused in my writing, as in my life, of rushing, of not waiting to describe in any generous way details that would chronologically set the scene. I move quickly from moment to moment and share little. This is what made returning to him for dose after dose so unexpected. In a novel that I read not so long ago, long textured descriptions preceded any lovemaking. Before the couple in question kissed, I was privy to the rise and fall of chest and breast, to the direction of the soft breeze that through an open window shifted the flames of candles dotted about the room. Before the bodies tangled, I was introduced to the fine chinoiserie of the wallpaper, the way the early evening fell on the various objects in the room, pale light glistening off the ochre clay on which the gold of gilded furniture was burnished, and to the tiny noise the ungreased mechanism of the door lock dared to make when it was turned. I even knew the way cigarette smoke moved about the bedroom to evoke old memories and sexually charge the ones in the making. It hung thickly, menacingly, in some parts of the room.

Unlike this slow measured way of being in the world, I've been criticised for taking everything at such close range that my pixilated representations reflect only a disorientating immediacy. 'It all happens far too fast and he's rather too stingy, and he will eventually have to write more than a short story,' one critic mused.

The French writer and vagabond, Jean Genet, observed that people introduced to sex at a young age are serious and hard minded. I agree. We do not have the inclination for foreplay. We do not open our mouths to tell long stories or toil away with descriptions that postpone the inevitable … 'the temperature in the room was this …' or 'before the first touch I experienced a longing I would attribute to that …'. No. For each orifice is alert and ready, or worn out and in retreat. Fulfillment of the other is our *raison d'etre* and this is best done without luxury or waste of time. There is no slow reveal. Courtship is, at best, 'the beginning of the end' as they say, and, at worst, a space where dialogue—a dialogue between—is expected. Do not ask us anything, ask *of us* what you will, but we will not speak.

Cultural theorists might say that we become what we are through repetition, the notion of performativity, an *over-and-over* that cannot be easily undone. Plugged up and mute at an early age, don't now ask us anything. Our skin has been doused with the astringent of submission and in retreat, pores close. We are penetrable only in so far as to wait would be a greater discomfort. A lemon reaches ripeness and readiness then it falls. A pomegranate opens and shows its glistening red and ready interior while still on the branch. In what way will I be taken? Plucked how? With him I existed in the space between; at once falling of my own ripe readiness and at the same time clutching at the branches of a trusted domesticity, but with my legs open.

'I like making a slut out of you,' he told me a few weeks in. This amused me. 'Mate, I was a slut when you were in short pants,' I said back, though he wasn't listening. He never really listened. Even in the face of my own desire and need, I was always able to resist just enough to double back on myself and lift my neck from the block and answer back. Like a helix, I performed an uncanny twist that allowed me to lean out over the precipice of my yearning, to lean so far out I might almost fall to my death inside him and rest, and at the same time to pull back, pulling away from how he constructed me.

Gaslighting is the process of psychologically manipulating someone into doubting their own sanity. Catfishing and gaslighting must make happy bedfellows, both snuggled together under a blanket of control and deception. He was a champion at both. But why was I such easy pickings? When he arrogantly disregarded me, why did I dart back to the places where I watched myself being duped? Why was I the object rather than the subject?

I knew love. I had love. My mother nurtured and loved me well. As with most mothers, she was the centre pin around which the spokes of family life radiated. It was an ambivalent centre however and perhaps where I learned the great skill of scratching about for love in uncertain ground. For example, she had a domestic nickname (only used by her sons in the house) which was at once warm and insulting, but which she tolerated, La Mooty.

She had worked as an *au pair* in Paris as a young woman and spoke French well. She often addressed us collectively as *le petits enfants*, called us for dinner saying *le dejeuner*, or would say *merde* when something unwanted suddenly happened about the house, for example, when the cigarette she'd placed, lighted end out, on the wooden kitchen bench so she could have both hands free to, say, crack an egg while she was frying breakfast, fell to the floor and left a burn mark in the boards. This happened so often eventually the floorboards took on a blemished uneven texture similar to her teenage boys' faces. The burns from the cigarettes posing as blackheads on the once smooth surface. I think *merde* was for the wasted cigarette rather than the pockmarked boards. So, *La* was recognition of the affinity she had to the French and *Mooty* was a take on the German word for mother *Mütter* (half our blood on dad's side was German) and used mostly by us boys as the slang 'moot', for vagina. So when all was said and done, when all was percolated down to its essence, she was her biology. When the tone was loving, La Mooty represented the nurturer, the hole through which we were birthed; when we were filled with teenage angst and desire, we used La Mooty in a libidinally charged way as we might dry hump her leg as we hugged her, a couple of humorous gyrations and say 'La Mooty, I love you' with a salacious extra 'oo' or two—she was the pleasure slit; and when we were angry, we spat the name at her, La Mooty, the cunt. But as I said, she tolerated it. She cared for us in the face of it.

When her kids were sick with tummy upsets, she encouraged us to purge. Holding me under my chin and around the throat she lent me forward over the side of the bed so my head was over a stinking plastic bucket that may have been used for any number of ghastly farm jobs in the hours before and told me to open my mouth. Her fingers, one with a large diamond-like stone on it, were inserted into my mouth and forced to the back of my throat until I vomited. Her fingers were long, but I guess too my throat then was shallow. Her nails, never painted but always well kept; her fingers smelt of a combination of cigarette smoke and scent (we did not call it 'perfume' as that suggested a liquid a little more common than what my mother hurriedly splashed on her wrists before she juggled children about, in and out of nappies, in and out of cots and beds, in and out of an old Holden Kingswood station wagon). I was going to say, 'an intoxicating combination of …' but at that time that was not true. The perversities of our childhood are, at the time they happen, of no consequence. It's later—as in my case at 14 years of age when two well-scented men smoking cigarettes approached me in the street and very politely, almost sheepishly, invited me to get into their car, that they begin to count.

I was promised lemonade once my stomach had been emptied, and in the upheaval of my system, I knew love. It was in the moment that she withdrew her fingers from my throat and removed the bucket of swill, saying, 'sleep now darling', and closed the bedroom door to shut me away from the rest of the family, that I knew I counted. As I grew older and suffered too much anxiety to get out of bed to go to high school, she reversed her tack of love and nurture, not emptying but filling me, as she'd gently knock on my bedroom door to tell me she was driving to the village and would I like a cream bun with jam and icing from the bakery to make me feel better? At about that time, she introduced me to sleeping pills to also help settle me. With Mogadon I was carried from worry. The joy of a little death.

☙

In 1979, the great country singer, Kenny Rogers, released the song *The Coward of the County*. The song tells the story of a man who never stood up and fought for himself; a 'yella belly' who became a man only after the love of his life, Becky, was attacked and gang raped by three brothers, local thugs, the Gatlin boys. It's a traumatic song, brutal themes and violent content. Nevertheless, it was played, as big hits are, on the 24-hour radio cycle. I was 10. At breakfast before school I listened closely to the words.

> There's someone for everyone, and Tommy's love was Becky
> In her arms, he didn't have to prove he was a man
> One day while he was working, the Gatlin boys came calling
> They took turns at Becky, n'there was three of them

School bag, lunch, chickens to feed, the dishes to be done and the table to be wiped, schoolyard friendships new and decaying even at that early age, the concerns and hopes for the day. The song made me sad but it quietly intrigued me too. '…*n'there was three of them*'. Three men, three aggressive hard men, hair on their arms, dirt under their nails. To see those Gatlin boys in action, to see their bodies move. To have them take turns of Becky, which back then was only a partially understood euphemism that I wanted to learn more about.

I erased Becky from the picture, leaving just enough of her to act as a conduit through which power, desire, brutality, touch and desperate longing passed. The movement of Gatlin arms, the hard muscle, the thrusts and the entitlement that propelled them remained. I inserted myself into the room. I watched. I smelled. The *mise en scene* of the moment truncated into the tiny little world of a boy's need. Any homely or domestic trace was removed. A flour sifter or a rolling pin on the bench or a chair pushed back from a table with the cushioned seat still warm—anything from Becky's kitchen—would have humanised and therefore wreck the scene.

After the brothers pulled up their pants, my identifications shifted and I had to account for Becky.

> Tommy opened up the door, and saw his Becky crying
> The torn dress, the shattered look was more than he could
> stand

I could not reconcile what I felt about Becky's pain with the feelings I had about wanting to be there as the Gatlin boys took turns. I could not separate or understand the places where violence, power and desire crossed over and sparked.

CB

'I don't tell people I'm gay, they don't need to know, it's not important,' he told me later when we had got to know each other a little better and the bisexuality ruse had ceased to hold any special flare. 'Gay is just a small part of who I am,' he was at pains to tell me. He regarded himself as superior for only showing a small blemish of what he thought had thoroughly damaged me. 'You gays, always in the pink zone—gay this, gay that, always putting it on parade and rubbing it in.' *Hares and Hyenas* he began to call me after a few meetings. This was an acerbic nickname that referenced the name of a local queer bookshop not far from where I lived. 'Listen, Hares and Hyenas, you keep doing ya gay life, ya gay job, ya gay partner, ya little gay dog, ya trips to Mardi Gras, and see how far it gets you.' He punctuated his spewl with, 'Don't you feel limited by all the *gay* shit?' He may as well have spat on the ground.

The reality that he seemed to have trouble grasping was that it *had* got me far and was shattering rather than engendering limitations on a good life. The triumph of nicely 'gay' life and long-term relationship with another man was something he found, if not repellent, at least confusing. Something he could not affirm. Being gay allowed me a critical eye that let me move through the world differently, allowed me to ask deep questions about the notions of desire and attraction, of pleasure and commitment. That forced me to very self-consciously claim who I am. And to critically think about where I was deepening the furrows of intergenerational history, and where I was contradicting them. It allowed me to rewrite family expectations and to wriggle out from under them. I think that's a great part of not being straight. He thought I needed something of a holiday from the pink zone and was doing myself a disservice by being too gay, too caught up, too much part of the 'community'.

'Listen mate,' I said to him, feeling a need to defend myself and others like me, 'if my neighbour goes to work at a building site in a blue tanktop and high vis, if he goes to the footy every Saturday to support his team, goes to the Bloke's World Festival interstate once a year and reverses a trailer around witches caps to win a prize, if he fucks his wife and on occasions stops off in a brothel in a faraway suburb on his way home, has kids and a dog, you don't criticize him for being too in the blue zone. You don't tell him to stop being so straight or that he needs to get out and expand his horizons.'

'Hares and Hyenas, you don't even know you're being played. A political pawn being moved about and you're too dumb to resist. They've got you by the pink bits and you don't even know it.'

I went to continue what I suspected was a futile defence, but he saved us both. Taking my hand, 'let's go have fun, let's look for another bloke, you know you want it, Poof.'

◌

In all posies some flowers last longer than others. Some drop their head and lose their colour while others stiffen up and stand tall. Once cut, some flowers continue to grow and new buds open. But at what point do you toss the posy away? Unsurprisingly, he was the type of person who could not tolerate even the slightest bruise or discolouration to how he had arranged me, and so binned me when he was done. Days passed without him turning up to the place we usually met, then weeks, then months. Slowly I scratched and picked at how I felt I had been used until it turned into a hard nub of resentment and a desire for retaliation and revenge. And I deeply missed him.

I put myself to bed for a number of weeks but rallied to stay strong. In my bookshelf were three linen-bound volumes I had never read, *The Complete Short Stories of W Somerset Maugham*. They'd been given to me after the death of a great aunt, and miraculously, after much culling of superfluous books, I still had them. For some reason, I opened them and began to read. The smell of old paper, rather than new plastic was reassuring: life is long and change is inevitable.

In Volume Two, quite some days into slothing about and feeling sorry, I came upon a marvellous story in which two writers are talking. One has been rebuffed in love and is moaning that he is broken and done for, that he will never recover. Tired of the whining, the other admonishes him and tells him to pull himself together and to write a story about it.

> 'You know, that's the pull a writer has over other people. When something has made him terribly unhappy, and he's tortured and miserable, he can put it into a story and it's astounding what a comfort and relief it is.'

But I found I could not write myself out of this one. I continued to fester and ruminate.

Then, without leaving the bed, I was saved by a dream that moved me towards understanding and softness. In the dream, Clifton Hill is a seaside suburb. My friend and I walk along the esplanade looking out to the watery horizon under which is the freeway, Hoddle Street and I guess the gay bookshop referred to earlier. We notice, as if for the first time, and say to each other how the landscape must have changed so incrementally that we had not noticed the coastline moving so far inland. Suddenly it just seems normal that children in bathers and sandy dogs are playing and running in the direction of Northcote.

As with the swirling timeframes of dreams, in the next moment it's the 1980s and I'm standing with an older leather queen in the bushes of the scrubby foreshore. He is very skinny and a bit gaunt, but handsome as. He looks scared. I lean forward to touch him but he pulls back. He undoes his fly nevertheless. No one says anything but the spectre of HIV is between us. He seems uncertain of my desire and approach. Distrustful. I am aware that I've gone back in time, and, because of it, know what the future holds. As he touches himself, I look into his face and see fear. There are deep wrinkles and worry lines around his eyes. I can tell he wants to move forward but does not let himself. 'In the future,' I say to him, 'we know that it's not our fault and we are not scared.'

His face crumples. Immediately he starts to cry, and I wake up.

Oppression is a ghastly taskmaster. Lateral violence is a bitch. Loneliness and longing are bastards. Shame makes a liar of all of us at some time or other. What we drag forward from the past retards us. When I was a child, my grandmother told my sister that if you place a piece of wedding cake under your pillow you will dream of the man you are to marry, and when we made apple pies with her she taught us to peel the green apples so the peel remained in one long string and then to toss it over our shoulder; whatever letter it resembled when it hit the kitchen floor would be the first letter of your husband or wife's name, she said. There was always an expectation that we would be happily coupled, married. That somehow without adequate inoculation, we would be immune to the foibles and complications of power and desire, of hope and history. It was a fantasy that never came true.

Henry von Doussa is a writer, visual artist and social scientist from Melbourne. He works for La Trobe University at The Bouverie Centre (Victoria's Family Institute) and The Australian Research Centre in Sex, Health and Society. The health and wellbeing of families, particularly when they are impacted by parental mental illness, is the current focus of much of his work.

GREETING CARD 4. ASHLEY SIEVWRIGHT

PETE
GAVRIIL ALEKSANDRS

When I was eighteen I bought drugs off a guy in the Blue Mountains named Pete. He was an ex-bikie and had been locked up for armed robbery for twelve years. He was forty-two, skinny, had goblin-like hair and blurry tatts. I was homeless and aimless in Western Sydney at the time. My father lived three doors away from Pete.

Before I went to score I'd check if my father was home so I could steal clothes, showers and nick his girlfriend's make up. I snuck a key from his sideboard when I was sixteen, the last time he let me in the house. That key was the gift that kept giving.

My father abused us all as kids but I liked to imagine I had a good life. I would get ready to go 'out' from wherever I was staying, drink cheap grog, play music and dance about. I would 'dress up', do my hair and feel pretty.

I guess it worked, I faked it till I made it. Pete treated me all top shelf.

He would take me on dates. He'd buy me lobster and champagne at the Penrith Leagues Club. He would wear a leather vest, jeans, a button shirt, trim his beard and smile showing a missing tooth. He whistled when he spoke, threw coins in the pokies and would give me a turn or ten.

Despite the posters of nude women covering Pete's lounge room walls and the porn lying around his house, I think part of him was genuinely looking for romance. He could be very funny and sweet, good company with stories a mile high. He never touched me once. He said he thought I was 'really fancy'.

I wasn't at all.

Pete's house looked like a tip. Sometimes I would sleep in cluttered rooms on his floor and it stank, but he always set up some sort of a bed. He would find clean sheets even though he never slept in clean sheets himself. He would run around, *no, no, stay there, wait, I will sort this out*!

Pete had a homeless friend camping in his driveway in a broken-down car. Pete cared where it mattered sometimes. I noticed this when I was tired, lost, and it mattered to me too.

We would smoke bongs together after I scored. He'd give me speed and we'd talk for hours. Mostly we talked about music as it played on his tape deck. Once we got past Cold Chisel or ACDC, Pete would play old jazz. He loved Nina Simone and would listen to her, gazing at his feet while his eyes moistened up. He liked to think we spent 'cultured' time together.

He laughed at 'poof jokes' but thought cops were scum. He knew I was a 'dyke' but he courted me anyway. It was really old-fashioned stuff.

He told me once that because I wasn't interested in him sexually it brought out 'the best in him'. I think it did too because the bits of him that liked me were largely absent of beasts.

Otherwise Pete was a real prick. He said awful things about his wife. I bet none of it was true. I never knew her. He only ever called her 'cunt'. I have no doubt he was a terrible father just like mine. He forgot his son's name.

Some nights he would set alight planks of weatherboard and rubbish lying around his house to make a 'cosy fire'. We would sit there, the lesbian, the bikie and a speaker out the window playing Nina Simone or Sarah Vaughan, sometimes Coltrane too. I never knew how a bikie found this music.

Pete would throw beer bottles over his shoulder in the backyard as he drank in his favourite chair, and fuck he sunk the piss. He'd suck alcohol from bottles like it was oxygen in an oven.

There was a pile of glass behind him, metres high towering above his fence. The mound would shine and sparkle like a frozen waterfall.

It was spectacular.

Over the top.

Self-punishing.

I knew underneath this pile of shattered glass Pete's heart beat somewhere. There had to be one. He loved me, I was totally unobtainable, gay and all.

One night tripping on acid at his place, with my hands held against another fire, I considered looking for Pete's heart in that gleaming mass. But I knew if I had tried to find it, I would have bled to death.

Gavriil Aleksandrs is a Melbourne based transman with a social work/social policy background who enjoys writing non-fiction, fiction, essays and poetry in equal measure. Gavriil has been published in *Archer*, *Dumbo Feather*, *Parity*, Affirm Press, a range of queer grassroots publications and in guest blogs. Gavriil has co-authored academic articles and social work texts on LGBTIQ+ mental health issues, homelessness and informal care giving in queer communities.

BORING
LIONEL WRIGHT

In Oregon USA they have a town called Boring. It has a twin city in Scotland called Dull, and a competing city in Arizona that takes away a portion of their most depressed tourists (the ones seeking the most appropriate location to suicide), called Why. Every newspaper editor in the Oregon region delights in headlining each morosely mundane mishap and murder that Boring offers up: 'Boring Child Dies', 'Boring Car Crash, Drug Use Suspected' and 'Boring Arsonist Claims Life of Fascinating Celebrity'. But the Boring community is also known for its annual 'goth float' every August on the Clackamas River.

And it was here I was living my backpacker dream with my new Mexican-American boyfriend Miguel. We were to don black swimsuits and heavy charcoal eyeliner, and alongside Wednesday Addams and Robert Plant lookalikes, rehearse our run in lurid pink donut-themed inner tubes. It was just under two weeks away. It would be the final adventure of my American holiday between university semesters, and I wanted to be sure our cheap blow-up chocolate and strawberry donut rings of air wouldn't sink from the weight of our props. I wanted to get interesting photos.

Miguel had asked me to practise painting the white skull of a Day of the Dead skeleton on his face, using a black and red flowered background along its edges, so he could bring some authentic *el Día de los Muertos* energy to the mostly Western goth brigade. I'd done a reasonable job by following face-painting plans from the internet, holding my phone against his endearingly sticky-out-y ears as I copied the outlines of the patterns onto his cheeks and forehead. He was now practicing applying black and green glitter to the shaved left half of my hair as I straightened up my floor length grim reaper cloak and tested the weight of the sickle from the costume shop when balanced against my donut ring.

'It doesn't look like it will burst,' I affirmed, 'I think it's going to hold.'

A 'ping' sounded from his pocket as he squeezed the tube of glitter into his hand, and though he tried to ignore it, it pinged again, and then again. And then again. He wiped the glitter onto his jeans,

rolled his eyes in his deeply expressive way, then pulled out his
iPhone.

'It's *mi hermana*, Juana, my sister,' he said, looking down onto the
screen through black circle painted eyes. He read the first part of
Juana's text: 'I've booked you the next free flight back to El Paso,
Texas: get yourself to the airport'.

He dropped the green glitter tube absentmindedly as he read on in
silence, his plum-coloured mouth momentarily agape. Then his
mouth closed into a thin white, determined line, as though the black
stitching I had painted across it sealed the white bone onto bone. I
had never seen him stand so still before; Miguel was always flowing
gracefully, like the waters of the Clackamas. Finally, he looked at me
and shook his head. 'One of *mis primos*, my cousin, has just been shot,'
he explained, 'but he's refusing to see a doctor.'

Miguel probably had enough skills, even though he had stopped
midway through his nursing studies to take a janitorial job at a school
and pay down some of his mounting student debt, to be the most
promising member of his family to supply some kind of help to the
cousin. This needed to be done without alerting any of the authorities,
he asserted grimly. '*Me tengo que ir de inmediato …*' he slipped
distractedly into his native tongue again, and then shook his white
skull face and held up a hand. 'I have to leave immediately, we have to
get back to the hotel! I want to pack up and book a car. Before the
family get desperate and take him to the hospital. Before *los policías
blancos* find him.' I noticed he never once told me his cousin's name as
he said all this. It was as though I too, *el chico blanco*, could not be
trusted.

'Welcome to the USA in 2019, *Niño australiano*.' Miguel smiled sadly at
me. We had taken an Uber back to the hotel room we'd splurged on
for the last weeks of my trip. He was still quickly shoving his shirts
and condoms away into his zip-up bag. I admired his squat, muscled
physique as it moved, like a dancer's, but shorter. He kissed me
chastely goodbye, on the lips, and then pulled back to look at me.
'Now you know the truth of it: that nothing is more quintessentially
American in the Trump era than being wounded in a mass shooting at
a Walmart by a white terrorist for supposedly being a bad *hombre*, and
then going to hospital where you end up $30k in debt and then hauled
away to be deported by ICE.' I looked away, feigning offense or
maybe disagreement that such an outcome could be inevitable if he
didn't leave now, shrugging my slight shoulders half-heartedly.

I'd run out of the money needed to return with him to El Paso, having pre-paid all of our adventures to the limit of my credit card and having just bought a fortnight of food from my remaining cash for the room the day before. Miguel had said it was foolhardy to spend everything upfront, that I was young and silly, that I didn't realise how things could turn on a dime. I hadn't listened. I'd wanted Miguel, so badly, to stay there with me for the fortnight before I returned to Australia probably never to see him again. I was being irrational.

'*Qué?*' He tried to catch my eye, shaking both my shoulders. '*Qué?* What? You're not even going to look at me now? You're not going to kiss me back?'

I craned my neck to pull my face further away from his still, showing no more maturity than my mere twenty years and knowing it. I took a deep breath in, masked as a moody sigh, to absorb his *vel Rosita* laundry scent mixed in with spice, coffee, sunlight and face-paint.

I thought about how I'd wanted to see his black glitter Lycra onesie with the skeleton on it wet from the white water splashing around the tube, hugging his thick body's lines. I'd wanted to hear his hysterical laughter half drowned out by the joyful screams of strangers. I'd wanted to make him take arty shots of me staring moodily into the distance with my grim reaper cape draped over the sprinkled pink donut's edge into the muddied Clackamas, for people we would never meet to 'like' on my Instagram page. I'd wanted to watch his black-stitch mouth finally return my far too quickly, far too frequently and shamelessly proffered 'I love you'. I'd hoped it would finally happen over a romantic candlelit dinner on one of our last Boring nights together.

'*Oh Dios! Eres tan niño* … you're crying! You're such a baby, he's not *your* cousin,' Miguel half-laughed at me, but his teeth flashed like fangs on the word *cousin* and then his lips thinned tightly over them. His chin jutted. I'd seen that face before, on boys at school, before they punched. Some tears that had broken free from my eyes were betraying me, so I swore, 'Fuck, I'm crying for you, not him!' and pushed away from him. I tried to point out that the El Paso sector CBP and ICE had just released a statement to the television news. 'Look, Miguel!' I exclaimed. The uniformed men on the screen were saying they would not be going to the hospitals, shelters, or reunion station for the El Paso Walmart shooting. I pointed at the screen, 'Your cousin will be perfectly fine without you, Miguel, but I won't be! See? Look, the authorities are encouraging anyone affected to seek medical attention! It's safe, he'll have the world around him, it will all be on camera, but I'll have nobody …'

Miguel rolled his huge brown eyes up me incredulously, 'Oh honey. Really? You believe these men? Sometimes you really are so selfish, so fucking stupid, *tan jodidamente estúpido*'. His words stung. A fresh wave of tears came as he hitched his black leather travel bag over his left shoulder. He stared at me, suddenly every one of his six years my senior. His eyes reddened, his back stiffened and he turned away. 'Yeah right; of course! And the CBP and ICE also said that they were providing those children sanitary conditions in their camps. There was literally a settlement from the 1990s, Flores, requiring them to do so … They *ignored* it, honey'.

I reached out an arm towards him meekly, and began 'But this time …' He turned suddenly and sliced through my sentence with a merciless chop from both his hardened brown hands before the words could even come. 'Lies have *consequences*!' His voice was building, and now he was almost yelling outright. 'These organisations no longer have the credibility to be taken at their word!' I sulked and he paused, momentarily sorry for me. But then he looked at me up and down, shook his head again and spat out: '… Even by … even by idiot white foreigners who know nothing! Wake up, Aussie boy!' He took his bag over to the door, opened it, then turned back towards me. 'Nobody will care that my cousin got shot. There'll probably be a second shooting somewhere else in the US within 24 hours, and any cover provided for Mexican men now by whatever this media program is right now …' he disdainfully flicked his fingers over his shoulders at the television screen beside him without even turning to look at it, '… will end. He will be just another bad *hombre* this side of the border, that Trump's base just want to get rid of. My cousin will be injured, but also trapped in debt and detention and then sent away, if I don't go to him right now. So I go, little boy. I go, because he is my family and at the end of the day nobody else will care. I go!'

I threw myself in a sulk onto our glitter-smeared, sex-stained hotel bed as Miguel turned and left. I dramatically turned up the cable news to drown out the goodbyes he softly called through the heavy door, after closing it. I let salty tears drip my mascara, eyeshadow and black lipstick onto my pillow. I felt some small satisfaction at the bitterly blackened sections of the formerly white material, a testament to my grief. I cried some more and then tossed and turned for a few hours into hot, defiant fits of sleep. I dreamed about Miguel with his loving family, his sisters and his cousins. I pictured Miguel stitching his cousin's wound. I pictured Miguel stitching his own lips in black thread across the white skull. And then stitching the hole that had gaped in my heart before I met him online, and that had started to gape again, now. And then I saw my own parents sitting white and cold at the dinner table, refusing to speak to me, after I'd come out during my first semester of the business degree they had pushed me into. I saw myself packing, or was it Miguel, a black leather bag. I saw myself running away from them all.

Hours later as I lay drearily on the bed in the darkening taupe hotel room, it became obvious that, of course, Miguel was right. He knew his own country, and after all I was just a guest in his wild land.

I sighed and flicked through my phone messages but there were no more from Miguel. I texted him weakly, 'I'm sorry. I know I'm selfish. I'm a 20yr old red-blooded white boy, thinking of nothing but making love.'

The newsreel of clips of the shopping centre where the El Paso mass shooter had appeared after posting a racist screed about a brown people 'invasion' on 8chan had been interrupted. A prim-suited woman with coiffed hair was now describing details from another, more recent incident. 'We're just getting word now that a gunman has killed his sister, and eight others, in a deadly mass shooting today …' she reported with a strange enthusiasm, 'in what was a tragedy for the Oregon district, Dayton Ohio'.

I flicked the screen of my phone over to the internet and found Donald Trump's Twitter page. His frowning orange face recurred beside a series of tepid responses to each unnamed instance of white nationalist terrorism. The most recent Tweet pronounced: 'Today, I authorized the lowering of the flags to half-staff at all Federal Government buildings in honor of the victims of the tragedies in El Paso, Texas, and Dayton, Ohio …' in his self-congratulatory style. Beneath this Tweet surged a wave of anger and vitriol from posters around the world. The top post was a reply from Bishop Talburt Swan, a black man pictured in white collared priest's garb with his arms crossed over his chest. He was calling out the USA as the only nation in the world where guns outnumbered people: 'There are 400 million guns in our nation,' his response spat at Trump's page, '… and all you're doing is sending 'thoughts and prayers'. You don't think or pray.'

I read through the posts, each declaring the author more tired of all the murders, and each declaring the author even more tired of their politicians' lack of action to prevent them. I felt ridiculous in my grim reaper outfit now, a child dressing up as death for laughs in a country

teetering at the edge of a precipice he didn't, he couldn't, understand.
I pulled off the cape and the gown, and threw them onto the floor.
Mum would be annoyed at my messiness, I thought. I leaned over and
picked them up, and then folded them into a neat black pile.

I opened a message dialogue on my phone for Miguel, and started
to type out: 'I hope your cousin is ok baby … I really really hope he is
not wounded too badly, that the killer didn't shoot anything too …',
and then I remembered how careful Miguel had been about not
mentioning his cousin's name to me. I couldn't know who would
open his message bank, on the other end of that line. I guess I didn't
really know that gorgeous man at all. And I guess he was right, I was
indeed a danger to him.

I deleted the sentences.

When I texted him again, the only image I allowed onto my screen
was a single small green speech bubble containing the red heart emoji.
Miguel didn't need to waste his time on hiding stupidly revealing
messages from some Aussie backpacker he'd only met in person a few
weeks ago, on today of all days.

I got out of bed to freshen up in the small gloomy white
bathroom, leaving my phone on the bed. I took the soiled pillow case
with me to wash the charcoal stains off in the sink, and caught sight
of my miserable black-streaked face in the mirror. I looked foolish,
thoughtless. Young.

I wondered in disbelief at the possibilities presented by two mass
shootings in the same day. Both came only one week after a different
man had also fired on a garlic festival in Gilroy, California, killing
three people and wounding 12. I remembered how all of the 8chan
killers had released posts calling on others to join them in shooting up
civilian areas. Was a coordinated alt right network planning and
executing these attacks globally? Were these uncoordinated responses
coalesced from a single seed we'd not yet understood? Was there
some kind of *behavioural contagion*, like how a queer boy's suicide
mentioned in the media of my small Western Australian rural town
had apparently inspired others to harm themselves in Tasmania and
Queensland?

Or was it a Stand Alone Complex; individuals acting in unrelated
but similar manners, offering the illusion of coordination?

For one reason or another, white supremacist male violence was
repeating itself, in location after location after location after location.
There were tiny differences in the faces of the victims—here a gay
Latino, there a Muslim woman, there a black man.

But the structure of their supremacist violence was always the same, like in an internet meme. And its success was scored by the media's reported body count.

I sneered at the news woman. *Everyone seems to play their part in this thing, whatever it is.*

From the bathroom I heard the crisp ping of my phone: a message! Miguel's painted face appeared again in my mind as my heart leapt, and I grinned to myself in the mirror despite the dried salt of my earlier tears. Perhaps all was forgiven! I ran over to the phone and picked it up.

The message was not from Miguel; it was from Mum. I opened it, melting into a relief that surprised me. I had not had a single word from her since I had moved into a share house with other uni students a few months ago, after coming out to her. 'Darling, your father and I are worried about you! Where are you?' The text read. 'Are you still in El Paso? We heard you were travelling there from your housemates. Everyone has been trying to contact you. We need you to call us right now! Please, let us all know that you're ok!'

Somehow, I had not expected her to say that. I guessed that the shootings had now hit the Australian news. I was not like all the other travelling millennials I'd met, mostly straight kids, still living with their parents and probably frantically responding to their worried Facebook messages this very moment. I was the loner, the prodigal son, looking for a new family in every strange man's face. Mum's fear I was dead in an American shopping mall felt so ordinary and so like what any young man would have to deal with in the same situation, that it was almost boring, in the strangest and most exciting way. I pressed my finger on the image of her sweet round face, to place a call to the house. It was maybe still, and it would maybe always be, my home.

Lionel Wright is an emerging queer writer studying an arts degree at a university in Melbourne. He has been blogging a backpacking trip around Asia and the Americas, and this will be his first officially published piece. Lionel is an adrenalin junkie who likes trialling strange sports, loafing about and getting lost in unusual locations, and meeting mysterious men.

KIM LEUTWYLER

American-born Kim Leutwyler migrated to Australia seven years ago. The Sydney-based artist interrogates beauty, gender and queer identity in a variety of media, with a focus on painting that confronts its primarily masculine history in the western art canon. Her works intersplice realist portraiture with abstractions, pattern-work and the prehistoric in ways which defy simplistic categorisations. They have featured in multiple galleries and museums throughout Australia and the United States. Leutwyler has been awarded many prizes over the years and in 2019 alone was a finalist in: the 2019 Archibald Prize for her portrait of Ghanaian-Chinese openly queer actor/broadcaster/writer/DJ and friend Faustina Agolley; the Portia Geach Memorial Award for her portrait of Trixie Mattel; the Naked & Nude Art Prize for her portrait of 'Sally'; and the Australian LGBTI Awards for her portrait of 'Heyman'. Additionally she was a semi-finalist in the Lester Prize Salon des Refusés and Doug Moran National Portrait Prize. Leutwyler holds concurrent bachelor degrees in Studio and Art History from Arizona State University, and additionally graduated from the School of the Art Institute of Chicago with a Painting and Drawing degree. Her originals and prints can be enjoyed and purchased at: https://kimleutwyler.com/

OPPOSITE PAGE: FAUSTINA. KIM LEUTWYLER

DANVOS. KIM LEUTWYLER

COLE. KIM LEUTWYLER

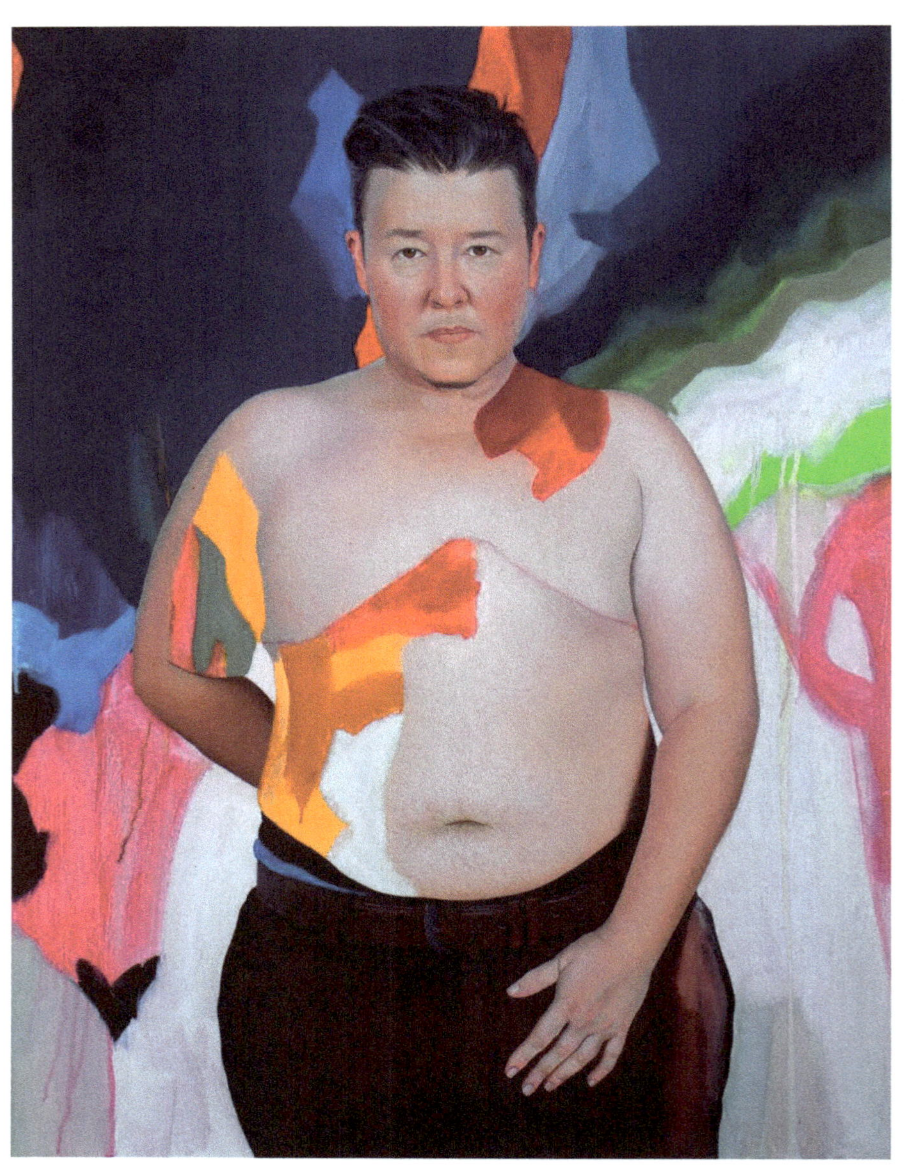

T CHICK. KIM LEUTWYLER

OPPOSITE PAGE: TAMARA [DETAIL]. KIM LEUTWYLER

CIRCUMSTANCES BEYOND OUR CONTROL
JOHN BARTLETT

ZOË

I'd finished stacking the dishes on the draining board when I first
noticed the palms of my hands were red and itchy. Nath was out, had
another special job on, Ralph was staying over at a mate's so it was
just me and Samantha home for a change. My hands were aching too.
I must be allergic to that new detergent I'd bought at IGA on a whim. I forgot
all about my allergies after Nath got home, but a few days later when I
was at work it happened again.

I was working a late shift and the train was coming into Waterloo
when I got the SMS from Samantha: *Mum, come home, cops here with
Ralph.*

I calmly made an official conductor announcement on the train
and held my breath: *Ladies and Gentlemen, unfortunately there will be short
delay due to circumstances beyond our control. I do apologise for any inconvenience.*

There's never a prescribed formula for this sort of situation so I
just made it up as I went along. It was all pretty easy. I explained to
Roger the driver and he radioed ahead for a new conductor. Rage
contained is unemotional when you are as used to it as I am, what
with two moody teenagers and, oh yeah, a husband who doesn't say a
lot. I only had to wait about ten minutes to get the other train back
into the city from the opposite track.

I tried phoning Nath but he must have been on a job, his phone
was switched off. So I phoned Samantha back and she said the police
were waiting until I got home.

I couldn't believe how bloody calm I was. Hah! 'Circumstances
beyond our control', nice easy words to describe a stuff up at home. I
knew Samantha would call only if it was a real emergency.

Ralph had been caught shoplifting at the local Safeway's that
afternoon. He'd been stacking shelves there during the previous
holidays. The manager knew him and didn't want to lay charges, just
got the police to bring him home to give him a fright.

I think that worked but Nath needed to be there too. Ralph took
more notice of his father. They were both risktakers at heart.

Nath never turns his phone off when he's working in case it's
another job. So where the hell was he?

NATHAN

I know you'll never leave her.

Rob's comment was perfect timing—post-coital I think is the
official term. A real kick in the balls—painful and accurate. I tried to
think of a smart-arse answer but nothing came to me.

He went to sleep then anyway as he sometimes did afterwards, his
meaty leg slung over mine. I had to get back to work soon but I liked
lying back in Rob's big Queen size bed after we'd been on the job—
all that damn space. We only had a double at home and Zoë and I
were always banging our arms and legs against each other, scrabbling
for room. Here I had a bit of peace for a while, the afternoon
shadows from the blind crisscrossing Rob's naked body.

He didn't have a perfect body. His smooth stomach was marred
by the scar of a botched appendix job and his cropped hair was
already greying at only thirty-five.

It had always been more than just lust with us. We talked and we
laughed a lot too. I'd come to need something he gave me as much as
I needed Zoë. *Needed or wanted?* I wasn't sure. But when there was this
urge, it sure dominated everything.

Zoë didn't seem to need or want me as much after the kids came
along. Mostly she was one independent wound up dynamo, until she'd
crash from work or the kids. I had no plans to leave them. I still loved
her; we'd been together almost twenty years and even learnt to
tolerate each other's faults. That was some accomplishment. *Wasn't
that real love?*

Reluctantly I dragged myself out from under Rob and went in
search of my overalls and jocks abandoned earlier on the floor. My
phone showed five voicemail messages. It was only when I'd left the
flat and was back in the Ute that I saw that three were from Zoë.

ROB

He'd always go back to Zoë. I knew that. The question was, was it
worth my being his bit on the side? The trouble was that Nathan
really made me laugh in a good sort of way and I'd always had the
hots for guys with a sense of humour.

Once the fucking was over there had to be something else. Sex with Nathan was a blast, no worries. Sweaty and intense but I often came too quickly.

The funny stories he told me afterwards about dickhead clients, lying beside him with my head resting on his chest, were more about feeling close to someone you trust, giving each other something we needed. He reckoned Zoë never had time anymore to listen to him, so I was his agony aunt, but one with a dick and balls.

Was that enough?

ZOË

It was after the cops had left and when Ralph was sitting white-faced on the sofa that my hands started to ache again. I'd lost my cool with him, got a bit overexcited I guess and now there were these two bright red spots on the palm of each hand.

Then I'd felt a bit sorry for Ralph. I'd gone into the kitchen to give him space and start getting tea ready, but I had to stop cutting up onions because I scratched my hands so much I thought they'd bleed.

And of course a week later that's just what happened. Nath had a plumbing job over the border and was away for the night. Before he'd left, he read the riot act to Ralph, but with a patience I'd never managed with the kids.

He called from his motel in Albury while I was watching 'Dancing with the Stars' and when I tossed the mobile down on the sofa, my hands felt sticky. I turned on the main light and saw blood on the sofa.

Both my hands were red and wet with what looked like blood. I got a shock but didn't panic. They hadn't bled too much so I bandaged them up, took a couple of Panadol, went to bed early and as my old Mum used to say *hoped for the best.*

NATHAN

We'd never had that much time to spend together before; almost a whole twenty-four hours. Rob didn't need much convincing for me to swing by his place. He had the afternoon off school and lived just off Sydney Road so it was on my way.

A hot north wind was blowing across Coburg, dust and plastic bags scudding tree-high so it was a relief to clear the city for broad paddocks and my Ute eating up the ks like it should. I knew Rob liked R'n'B so along the Hume we soaked up Billy Boy Arnold and Junior

Wells—'Don't stay out all night' (even if I was) and 'Vietcong Blues',
stopping only at a South Albury pub for a beer.

Listening to someone else singing the Blues was easier than talking
about us, about where it was all heading. We mostly managed to avoid
that topic. Maybe we were just smart, living in the moment, or
cowards, evading the question.

I dropped Rob off at the motel and went to check out the job I'd
be doing the next day. He was a bit pissed off being abandoned, *What
am I supposed to do, just sit around the motel pool in my little red speedos and
suck off a few truckies?* I couldn't take the risk of us being seen together.

That was the trouble with Rob. He was too *out there* for my liking.
Unpredictable, too. It was always easy for him, but *not for someone in my
situation.*

This would only work if we flew under the radar.

ROB

That night away in Albury showed up a few cracks in our
'arrangement' as Nathan euphemistically described our situation.
Everything for him was just 'cool' if it was all discrete but being in
public together made him very nervous. He preferred to hide me away
like one of Bluebeard's wives.

The tiles at the end of the motel pool were scorching against the
soles of my feet. I swam a few laps. It felt like swimming in cool
lemonade and not a horny truckie in sight.

It'd serve Nathan right if I did go off with someone else.

Then for some reason, I started thinking about Zoë whom I'd
never met. I sliced through the water of the pool—a melting
dreamland of distorted shapes.

It was a cliché I'd never say out loud but I'd really fallen hard for
Nathan. Zoë knew nothing about me but that still didn't make it OK.
If she ever did find out about us I could imagine her pain. I'd feel that
sort of pain too if he ever went back to her.

True, I was a lapsed Catholic. But I still had an idea of what was
right and wrong.

After about twelve laps I calmed down. I was still no clearer about
what to do. Funnily though, after I'd got out of the pool and was
drying myself, I noticed how sore the palms of my hands had become,
aching, itchy and bright red.

Too much bloody chlorine in the pool.

Time for a shower and a change before we grabbed a bite to eat. Who knew if I'd ever have Nathan to myself again for another twenty-four hours?

RALPH

I freaked out when Mum woke me up and got me to ring the ambos. Her hands were bleeding and she couldn't stop the flow.

Sam and I went with her to the hospital. Dad was away overnight. I was the man of the house, for once. That felt good.

In the end they sent her home after a couple of hours. They said it was nothing physical, nothing to worry about. It sometimes happened when people were too stressed. One of the nurses told me, while another nurse was bandaging Mum's hands, that it was called stig-something.

Dad's gonna be surprised when he gets home. He'll just say what he always says to me: *Shit happens, just deal with it.*

Suddenly there's a lot of shit for our family to deal with. *But my ol' man will know what to do. He always does.*

John Bartlett: is the author of three novels, *Towards a Distant Sea*, *Estuary* and *Jack Ferryman: Reluctant Private Investigator*, as well as *All Mortal Flesh*, a collection of short stories and *A Tiny & Brilliant Light*, his published non-fiction. His poetry has been published in a number of Australian and overseas journals. In June 2019 Melbourne Poets Union published his Chapbook *The Arms of Men* as part of the Union Poet Series Chapbook. In 2020 Ginninderra Press will publish a full collection of his poetry.